The FAILURE Project

The Story Of Man's Greatest Fear

ANUP KOCHHAR

B&S
Body & Soul Books

ISBN 978-93-52015-78-8

Cover: Fravashi Aga
Layouts: Chandravadan Shiroorkar, Leadstart Design
Printing: Thompson Press

First published in India 2016 by
BODY & SOUL BOOKS
An imprint of
LEADSTART PUBLISHING PVT LTD
Unit 25/26, Building A/1
Near WadalaRTO, Wadala (East), Mumbai 400037, INDIA
T + 91 22 24046887, +91 96 99933000 F +91 22 40700800
E info@leadstartcorp.com W www.leadstartcorp.com

To the thousands of people
who experience failure every moment.
The world has evolved because someone somewhere
experienced failure.

ABOUT THE AUTHOR

'More than success, failures have been the turning points in my life. They were also learning points leading to success. The first failure-milestone occurred when I failed to qualify in the pre-med exams. That led to my graduating in the life sciences from Delhi University. But those were the days when IT beckoned the brave. So I went on to professional education in Information Technology. It was the time of Y2K and the new millennium; an IT guy was worth his weight in gold. The millennium came, the stock markets crashed and the IT bubble burst.

Then came the internet boom. I visualized a world changed by e-commerce. So I seeded a web-commerce start-up. But the time was not right and the concepts and technologies were still developing; people were hesitant about transacting online. The start-up failed. I was then drawn to finance, the central axis of companies. This took me on a superhighway to the stock markets. I saw how ruthless and impersonal the markets are and lived through the crash of 2008. Stock markets have perhaps destroyed more people and economies than wars have done. Although I came to make a quick buck and leave, I am still here, analysing market trends.

From medical school aspirant to finance has certainly been a hell of a journey, with some spectacular failures. Each milestone provided me with insights into why we fail, how we fail, and the need to get up, learn and move on. It has involved direct encounters with more failures than successes. I have been mauled I must admit, and every encounter left its mark. Looking back, I feel those encounters were necessary. Certainly no one sets out to fail, but failures do happen. Every failure was a lesson that came in handy in the next venture. Every one of them happened for a reason.'

Anup can be reached at:anupmkochhar@gmail.com

CONTENTS

FOREWORD
The Greatest Fear Of Man

WHAT WOULD YOU ATTEMPT TO DO IF YOU KNEW YOU COULD NOT FAIL?

Close your eyes for a moment and think of the things you fear.

As you search deep within, a host of worries is likely to float up into your mind – the kids missing school, class projects, exams, not making the morning train, traffic jams, deadlines, board meetings, job interviews, competitions, a crucial match, keeping up relationships, and so on. These are perhaps the immediate fears that engage you through the day, but as you widen the scope, another hall of fear opens up. This time, more serious issues emerge – the future, your career, health and marriage. Broaden the perspective further and you get society and the environment.

Can you identify the common thread running through all these issues? The fear of losing out; the fear of not keeping up with life. Look closely and you will see them all devolve into a single fear: the *Fear of Failure*. All fears are but branches of the fear of failure. Restate your fears: the kids failing to catch the school bus, failing to make the morning train, failing to meet the deadlines at work, failing to maintain relationships, failing at career, failing health, failing marriage, failing social order, failing environment. Even the fear of death is fear of failing to continue life.

The fear of failure is not just the greatest fear of man, it is *the* fear of man. All other fears are avatars of the fear of failure.

Failure is capable of causing extreme mental and emotional anguish. It can destroy lives. Like fire, failure has the power to be destructive, but, if harnessed, can be channelled creatively.

Our lives are driven by two forces:

1. If I do this, I will get. [Positive force]
2. If I don't do this I won't get. [Negative force]

Often, our lives are driven by a powerful negative force. Fearing to fail becomes our primary motivation. Throughout our lives we find ourselves engaged in managing things so as not to fail. But failure happens, and will continue to happen. What is important is *how* we react to failure. Can we weather the pain failure brings? More importantly, can we channel the energy of the tsunami failure generates?

It depends. Most people find it tough to handle failure. Many people are unable to bear the pain. Depending on the magnitude of the failure, they feel devastated. But there are those who resist and use their greatest fear as a strong motivator to achieve their objectives.

INTRODUCTION
What Is The Failure Project?

What do we know of failure? More importantly, *how much* do we know? Everyone faces failure at some point. It is akin to a rite of passage. Some take failure as an experience to gain from, while for others failure means switching to self-destruct mode.

What is failure? What does it mean to different individuals? People have been searching for the ever-elusive Universal Formula for Success (much like the elixir of life). Society is obsessed with success and desires to keep failure at bay at any cost. But this dread of failure actually makes us more prone to the effects of failure. Is failure then a disease to be manically avoided, or can we put this affliction to good use?

Failure per se is not a disease but it can trigger anxiety, depression and even suicide. If failure can strike anyone, how can we handle it? Medical science has a well-defined mechanism in place for dealing with diseases – it identifies the symptoms and then prescribes a methodology for their management. Psychologists and Psychiatrists have management practices for dealing with anxiety and depression. But do we have a method for dealing with failure?

The Failure Project analyses failure in its numerous *avatars*. And attempts to answer questions like those above; possibly providing some answers. This is not a book about the virtues of failure, even though a chapter says we need to learn to fail. The point is we can use failure as a tool to get to our real objective i.e. happiness (those who thought 'success' need to go through this book right now).

In schools and universities, projects are defined as learning assignments and require a fair amount of research. Students are required to define and analyze the problem, devise their fact-finding mechanism, present their findings, and suggest solutions.

Sometimes though, a project gains great significance, requiring constant updations based on changing dynamics and understanding. It evolves into a programme and becomes an ongoing project. *The Failure Project*, which started off as an assignment to understand failure in its various dimensions, is, I believe, such a programme. Why? Firstly because of its significance; the manner it effects our lives. Secondly because of the newer dimensions revealed at every step we take.

As I moved on with my research I was surprised to learn about the positive effects failure can have on the human psyche; how some of man's greatest inventions and discoveries were founded on failure. As you read, there may be times you may feel that certain facts needed to be included or that some points require expansion. This is exactly what makes *The Failure Project* a programme – a project that keeps evolving. I invite you to be part of it and to send me your thoughts and insights into managing this frightful but peculiarly motivating force.

PART I: FAILURE HURTS

Success and failure are both difficult to endure. Along with success come drugs, divorce, fornication, bullying, travel, meditation, medication, depression, neurosis and suicide. With failure comes failure.
Joseph Heller, *Catch-22*

When faced with the pain of failure, giving up is an easy option. Tragic stories fill the newspapers every day, each tale more horrifying than the last. And each time we wonder: Why? What forces young people full of energy to take the extreme step of ending their lives? Why do they give in to despair?

The answer: Failure.

We have only ourselves to blame. We as parents, as teachers and as a society, are responsible. We, as a society, have laid down the laws of success and the consequences of failure. So strong is our obsession with success that it has become a matter of life and death in impressionable minds. What they should know instead is that failure at one stage is not the end of the world. There *is* life after failure. Life itself is a series of ups and downs. Failure can be turned into success. History is full of stories about society having dumped and labelled people as failures but who went on to become huge successes. In every field and profession, we see the same patterns. Of course, we have heard about them but we continue to believe *they* were different from us; that *they* were simply misjudged by society when, in fact, they were brilliant.

There is a very small difference between success and failure. There can be no doubt that failure 'just missed success'. Unfortunately, we live in a result-oriented society that is obsessed with the bottom line – net profits, success, awards and prizes. The end-result is all that matters. This thin line turns into a wide chasm dividing the winners from the losers.

But are those who lose really losers? This book is aimed at determining the role of failure in determining success. We read about famous people but we rarely think of the failures they encountered on their way to the top. As we shall see, failure is not a bad thing and is often an expressway to success. This is also a book that highlights the life of people who used their failures to their ultimate advantage.

1. HURTING

In the summer of 1990, in an upscale school in New Delhi, Sohum was crying himself hoarse. His friends rallied around but he remained inconsolable. Mrs. Kumar, the drama teacher, had pulled Sohum from the class play saying, "You cannot play the role properly." He was 8-years-old, studying in class IV.

February-March are tough months for school children in India. Many suffer from anxiety and medical help is often required to calm them. Some are treated for severe anxiety. This is the time when exam fever gains epidemic proportions. The months of May and June see a spurt in cases of depression, as well as suicide attempts, by 17 -18 year-youngs. Some of them succeed.

Let us accept it – failure hurts. Even minor failures (if there is such a degree of relativity), are capable of causing deep hurt. Failure is like flu. It can happen to anyone. Just as it is difficult to find a person who hasn't had the flu, it is difficult to find someone who has not been stuck by failure at some time.

Can we quantify failure in degrees and say, 'on a 10 point scale this failure causes this much pain?' Extremely difficult. A student who has studied hard but failed, will be as devastated as a sales team that has worked hard but failed to clinch the deal. A failed relationship is no different. But, to a student who has not paid much attention to his studies, failure will not generate the same level of pain.

What does failure do to us? We fall into a vicious downward spiral. Failure is a lot like a shot from a double barrel gun but with a difference. The first shot is like the news which explodes in one's face. But it is the second, after a short time lag, which causes the most damage. It comprises of pain, humiliation, shame, frustration and anger. The first shot pales in comparison. It is life after the blast that causes the most hurt.

One of the most visible changes failure brings to our psyche is that it makes us cautious. The fear of failing again slows us down. Even the failure experiences of others are potent. Accidents are all about failure: of man or machine or both. They are an easy benchmark to measure the effect of failure. Witnessing an accident or even hearing about one, makes us more compliant to traffic rules. We consciously slow down at crossings. Bikers who generally avoid wearing helmets quietly strap them on. Car travellers buckle up.

However caution can easily lead to over-caution and kill confidence. This loss of confidence brings about a lowering of our own self-worth (SeW). We begin to see ourselves as incapable of succeeding. Lowering of SeW impacts our whole attitude towards life. We begin to focus on the negative aspects of everything: failure, death, finding fault with the system, with individuals, indulging in incessant criticism; finally ending with a pessimistic psyche. It also affects our social life. Low SeW robs us of courage to pursue social interactions, leading to withdrawal, which further triggers self-neglect, when we think there is no point in self-development. We put our personal interests on the backburner, giving priority to others. While this aspect may seem altruistic, it is actually self-destructive. Slowly we reach the point when we lose all respect for our own opinion and live in eternal doubt. Finally, we conclude nothing can be done and that there is no point in continuing to live – and take the ultimate step.

2. FIR: FIRST INSTANT REACTION TO FAILURE

Imagine: A student failing his exam, an athlete losing a race, a cricket team crashing out before the bowling attack, a football striker missing a goal. What are the first thoughts that come to mind when you hear of someone failing? Irresponsible, lazy, no good, fool, no future, poor training, loafer, serves him right, needs to be given a kick...if these are your FIRs (First Instant Reactions), then you are not alone. First thoughts usually involve finding fault with the person. The fault finding scenarios may expand to include his methods, character, friends and even his upbringing.

Few of us pause to consider scenarios which may have been key factors in his failure. Few sit back and reflect on the real issues causing young people around us to fail and still fewer engage our minds with what to do about those moving about with the stigma of failure stamped all over them like open wounds oozing blood.

Now, the second exercise: Consider a picture of yourself, failing. Do the same words that described a stranger failing at their tasks come to you? Or a different set of terms? I am betting they are altogether different. Most often, terms like 'lack of opportunity', 'system faults', 'social inequality', 'favouritism', 'prejudice', 'racism', 'glass ceiling' and thoughts of self-pity, crowd in.

What causes the change in reaction? The fact remains that even after experiencing the pain of failure, the two lists remain separate. Why are we not sensitive to the pain of others? Why this apathy?

3. INSIDE THE MIND OF ONE WHO HAS FAILED

In a 100 meter race, eight top athletes are competing. Only one will be ecstatic as the winner. Two will console themselves with second and third positions. The other five will be inconsolable. That makes it a 62.5% failure rate. Consider a job scenario where 100 odd applicants send in their resumes for three positions. The failure rate shoots to 97%. Widen this scenario to medical entrance exams, where 200,000 students appear for 2000 seats. That is a 99% failure rate. While nobody denies the importance of the 1% who succeed, very little is said or done about the 99% who do not.

What happens to those five athletes who may have run the best races of their lives but did not qualify? Or the 97 who did not land the job they believed they were made for; or the 99% who lost out on pursuing their dream careers? For starters, they are condemned as 'those who failed' or simply as 'failures'. This failure tag has no age or gender limitations. Three year olds compete for nursery admissions prestigious schools every year and many fail to gain admission. They too, qualify for the F- tag. They undergo the same process of humiliation and trauma as an adult.

A failed result triggers two basic thoughts in the mind of the person – what he expects from himself and what society expects from him. A third thought often proves to be the most troublesome: His perception of what society thinks of him. The first can be dealt with by being honest with oneself and doing a self-evaluation. The second too, is manageable, for society quickly loses interest in failures. It is the third point, the perception of his own image in the eyes of others, which manifest as: 'What will people think?' or 'How will I face the world?' or 'What will I tell people?'This is difficult to handle and causes the most pain. It is perhaps the toughest battle we wage on our return, in defeat. Social conformity is strongest in Asian nations like India, Japan and Korea; in Western countries, the creed of individualism causes expectations from the self to take prominence.

Consequently, Western psychologists identify with the loss of self-esteem as the primary outfall of failure, with social pressure as second. In Eastern nations, social honour and prestige are the most valued. Understandably, apprehension of shame and rejection dominate, preventing minds from breaking away from traditional thinking. An important reason for the industrial revolution happening in the Western world was that inventions require an appetite for risk-taking; this translates into an equal ability to face failure. Inventions require different thinking which challenges the existing norms.

The Eastern world, with its high social conformity and low tolerance of failure, was unable to actively engage in the invention and risk-taking process and consequently lagged behind. Instead, they strengthened their value systems and traditional knowledge. This is the reason you are more likely to find heroic stories in the traditionally strong Asian cultures, about those who gave their lives for the community. The price of honour is certainly high. We need to appreciate that being different is not the same as being wrong. A 'wrong' answer is just a different answer, a different perspective which could be used to address the issue differently. Unfortunately, our obsession with the 'right' answer makes it difficult to see the importance of an alternative answer.

Why does failure hurt? And why does it affect people differently? Why are some people more likely to act rashly and pull the trigger? Why has there been a sudden increase in cases of suicide? More than the act of failing, it is the tagging that hurts; why insults sting. It is society that magnifies the hurt, causing us to stick to A and avoid B at all cost. Failure is a social taboo.

Social Status A	**Social Status B**
Accomplishment. Strength.	Shame. Defective. Incompetence.
Prosperity. Confidence.	**Negative.** Static. Misery. Faulty.
Positive. **Happiness.** Euphoria.	**Problems.** Ugly. Poverty. **Fear.**
Dignity. **Truth.** Continuity.	Passive. **Failure.** Disaster. Loss.
Beautiful and alive. Support.	Under performer. Defeat. **Chaos.**
Harmony. Winner. **Success.**	Ruin. **Weakness.** Lies and untruths.
Victory Performer. **Achiever.**	Death. Punishment. Loser. Frailty.
Win Honours. Peace	Frustration. Wrong. Fall. Mistakes.

We all want Status A and to avoid moving to Statius B.

We are people who need to be among people. The problem is that once we are among them, we feel compelled to sort ourselves into social hierarchies. If we were wolves, we'd fight to establish the social order of the pack. But since we are humans with outsized brains and language, we use words instead. It is the social hierarchy game that makes insults sting. We are wired so that it feels bad to lose social status and feels good to gain it. ~ William Irvine, Prof. of Philosophy, Wright State University.

4. BEING BRANDED A FAILURE

There is no harm in failing. While failure is certainly a disappointment and causes us to introspect on the causes, it's being branded a failure that causes the most pain; when 'failure' changes from being a verb to becoming a noun.

We need to substitute 'trier' for failure. The word 'fail' is closely related to the word *fall*. A child taking his first step falls, cries and then tries again. Why does he try again? Because he *wants* to, but does not, know the meaning of failure. As he grows up and does not perform according to the requirements of the system, society labels him as a failure. It is society that inflicts the most pain.

How does a child of six or seven, perceive failure or success? It is society – parents, teachers, relatives and neighbours, who together brand him a failure. And it is this branding that creates the fear of failure in him. Fear of being labelled a failure makes him cautious and robs him of the confidence to try. This branding affects even the successful. They chase success but not excellence, living in constant fear of failing. Even though they are successful, happiness remains elusive.

A young child sees the world through his elders' eyes. We, as a society, are responsible for creating the perception of success and failure. We tell our little ones what success and failure are, and encourage success with praise and clapping; failure to perform brings scorn and discouragement. But the fact remains that we cannot learn without failing.

In a class of 40 students, everyone has a different learning curve. Some students pick up things quickly while others take time for concepts to soak into their brains. The latter are often branded as slow learners. In our scramble to identify brilliant children, we can miss our Einsteins and Edisons. Einstein was labelled a slow learner while Thomas Edison's teacher said of him, 'You cannot do anything in life.'

Is it possible that the whole exercise of creating successful students has turned into a mechanism to judge *teachers*? Do teachers come under the scanner when students fail? Failure is a reality. Experts have designed systems to measure every aspect of our growth right from the pre-birth stage. They map development to a 'normal' behavioural chart to see if a child is underperforming or outperforming for his age; they decide if he is brilliant or slow.

It is good to believe in science and its methods. But even today we know very little about how the brain works and how exactly we learn. Newer discoveries by scientists have negated our earlier understanding. When we proclaim a child to be a failure simply because his rhythm does not match the norm, could it be that the map itself is wrong? Today, we know that children learn at their own pace and some are late bloomers. Expecting quick results according to a planned behavioural chart may not be fair to the child. Our scientific measurement of success may condemn a child to failure.

Here is an interesting example to illustrate the point. Some species of Chinese Bamboo show little signs of growth initially. For four years, season after season, it appears as a tiny shoot, just showing it exists. People are baffled. But in the fifth year, magic happens. The tiny bamboo shoot suddenly grows some *80 feet in a single year*. How do we explain that? How did the tiny non-starter suddenly gather steam and shoot up? It seems magical till you know the cause behind it. The Chinese discovered that bamboo is actually a fast growing grass. For four years, while the world is giving up on it, the tiny shoot is busy growing underground, developing a massive root system. Once the support system is in place, it shoots up. It is planned and scientific but we are unaware of how it works.

We want to see growth *now*, every day, so that we can measure and map it on our charts. In this hurried world of 2-minute noodles and instant coffee, we want to see our children performing as soon as they enter school and are willing to pay top dollar for that. But a child's brain is not motivated by thoughts of money; it has its own intelligence that often frustrates scientists.

We should understand a child may be building systems to support his knowledge tree. He has to be given time to nurture it before being branded and condemned as a non-performer. To a statistician, the bamboo shoot took five years to reach 80 feet. That is 16 feet a year, when actually it did not grow at all for four years. We *know* statisticians are often wrong in interpreting data, yet we believe implicitly in their findings.

Pictorial Representation of Success and Failure

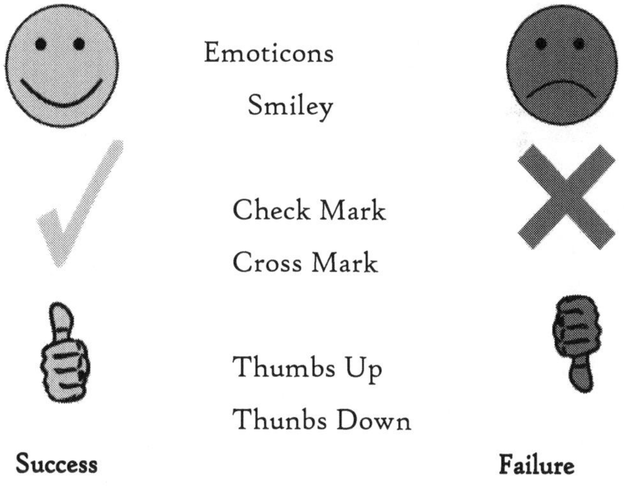

5. FRUSTRATION

In psychology, frustration is a response to opposition, anger and disappointment, arising from perceived resistance to the fulfilment of individual will. In other words, frustration is an emotional response to failure. American psychologist, Saul Rosenzweig, proposed three broad personality categories based on how we experience anger and frustration:

1. **Impunitive:** No punishment. Denies that failure has even happened or one's role in it. Since failure has not happened, there is no question of any punishment.

2. **Extrapunitive:** Other than yourself; meaning, blame it on others.

3. **Intropunitive:** Inside; take it on the self.

In short, the three types can be described as: Deny it/ hide it and blame it on others/ plead guilty.

While these are broad categories, in real life they can be stretched to form a spectrum, with the individual living in denial at one end, to putting the blame on others, and then taking it on themselves at the other end. Within these three broad categories, people respond to different situations differently, hence the categories do not typify a person, but the response. Anyone exhibiting a particular response is labelled accordingly.

The Impunitives are the incorrigible ones. You see them as the politicians who never admit their decisions failed, or the economists who believe their theories are fault-proof. They are the rich, powerful and overconfident people who believe they can do no wrong. They display traits of arrogance and apathy. They are also gullible, easily misled.

The Extrapunitives on the other hand, are the most common. You meet them everywhere, blaming everyone else but themselves. They are also the most vocal and spare no one a share of the blame. When they cannot find anyone, they blame the circumstances, nature, and even God. They are the blame-shifters, always looking for scapegoats; they create stories and distort facts to save their skins.

The Extrapunitives are more prone to hide their failures, brushing it under the carpet and hiding skeletons in the cupboard.

The Intropunitives are hyper-critical of themselves; once they fail, they harbour a long-lasting fear of failure. They sit on files, procrastinate and delay. They over-analyse a problem and often paralyse the decision-making machinery.

How do these three types react to the pain of frustration? The Impunitives behave as impervious, thick-skinned people. The Extrapunitives love to play *pass the parcel*, shoving the pain towards others. But it is the Intropunitives who we really need to worry about. They are the ones who are hypersensitive to the pain of failure and are deeply affected by the shame and humiliation that failure brings. They are the most susceptible to plunging into depression or inflicting self- injury.

On 4 September 2014, newspapers published the findings of a decade-long study by the World Health Organisation which said India was the suicide capital of the world (one in every three suicides takes place in India): *The report released today says that an Indian commits suicide every two minutes. In 2012, the WHO believes that 2.5 lakh people killed themselves in India. The government's estimates are significantly lower.*

'Young people appear most vulnerable (the maximum suicides in India were committed in the age group 15-29 years). More men kill themselves than women in India. There are indications that for each adult who died of suicide, there may have been more than 20 others who attempted suicide,' says Shekhar Saxena, lead author of the WHO report and Head of the WHO Department of Mental Health and Substance Abuse in Geneva.

'It is an extremely serious problem and is likely to increase in future because of rampant materialism in society, social economic and educational disparity, lack of access to healthcare etc.,' says Prof. MC Misra, Director, All India Institute of Medical Sciences(AIIMS), New Delhi. 'Recently, my own niece committed suicide, apparently for no reason,' he added sadly.

Prof. Misra is right in identifying the possible reasons of escalating suicides, but by his own admission he remains baffled by that of his niece. These factors apparently did not hold true in her case. Why? She had access to healthcare and material, social, economic and educational disparity, were likewise ruled out. So what was being missed here? What pushed her to crisis level?

PART II: THE FIRST ENCOUNTER

In school, you're taught a lesson and then given a test.
In life, you're given a test that teaches you a lesson.
Tom Bodett

The schooling system is our first major interaction with society. We learn the ways of the world and compete with one another. This is where we begin to learn and distinguish between what is right and what is wrong. We stand up to be evaluated, and evaluate others as well.

School is also our first major encounter with failure.

1. EXAMINATION HELL

No one likes to be evaluated and all exams cause stress. These are two established facts. Why? Exams bring candidates under scrutiny. Exams require them to *prove* their worth. It means that the other people do not accept your word when you say, 'I have mastered this art'. Your honesty is questioned and you must demonstrate your power/knowledge. It only when others have seen it that they believe.

The logical next step is to prove it your claim. But mistrust is the root of anxiety. 'Why can't they just believe me? I know this subject thoroughly, so why do I need to prove myself?' Seeking proof is examining a person. Exams are thus symptoms of a trust-deficit society. Exams are essentially a test of honesty and integrity, not of knowledge, skill, aptitude or attitude. The best exam would be the self-exam, where the candidate would examine himself. The system would have faith in him and trust his word.

But external exams are deemed essential, if only to check the honesty and sincerity of students. The education system applies exam controls at two points – to enter the education system, and to exit it. The controls for getting into the system are the entrance exams, such as those held for the IITs, medical colleges, and IIMs. The student is evaluated for aptitude before being admitted. It is like the security gate of heaven and people are checked for their life deeds. Those people who had led a righteous life may enter. But once inside, life is cool and paradise can be enjoyed.

The other form of evaluation is for exiting the system. There is a cross-bar at the end and students must jump over it to qualify. This control at the exit is used for mass education programmes. Imagine a race where everyone is invited. Thousands begin the race. Some dropout at various stages having covered some distance, but only those who finish get a certificate. The objective is to encourage people to run – all the way.

The 10+2 system in India is designed for mass education. Getting in is easy. People are encouraged to get their children educated. At the end of the period, there is an exam for getting out – the Board exams. At the professional level, programmes run by organisations like the Institute of Chartered Accountants of India, are those with gates at the end. Exams at the exit level test for transmission of knowledge while the entrance exam tests aptitude. But no exam can measure the intelligence, wisdom and abilities of students in a few hours.

So which control causes more stress, more pain? Struggling to get in or get out?

In the exit situation, the student is already in the education system and has gathered knowledge. If he fails, he can understand his shortcomings and overcome them the next time. But in the entrance situation, the student has an open-ended curriculum. He is apprehensive about getting in. Failing an entrance test is like being denied entry to heaven. Entry denied would crash any dreams of living in paradise. The frustration of being unable to reach heaven, having come so far, is tremendous. Also, entrance exams are competitive in nature. So, besides the frustration of missing the good life, there is also the pain of being defeated by other students. Exit exams are not competitive as they are meant to check if knowledge has been correctly transmitted. Exit exams therefore cause less stress than entrance ones.

But what if the exit exams become the eligibility criteria for appearing in another entrance exam? An exam to appear for another exam? The stress level is bound to increase. The annual exam ritual of *the Boards*, increases stress levels among students primarily because it becomes an exit *and* a pre-entrance exam. The marks attained in the first form essential criteria for sitting the second. A minimum of 75% marks, for example, are required to sit for the entrance exams for the IITs and medical colleges.

On 1 April 2010, the Right to Education Act came into force in India. Of the many fundamental clauses it had, was: *Every child between the ages of 6-14, shall have the right to free and compulsory education in a neighbourhood school, till completion of elementary education.*

The Act was to lower the dropout rate, increase the literacy rate and lower stress in the 6 – 14 age group. Most schools had a policy that anyone failing for two years would be pulled out of the system or could withdraw voluntarily (under pressure). With the compulsory education clause, it was no longer possible to do this. Schools interpreted the clause to mean: *All students of Std. I to VIII will be promoted to the next class irrespective of examination results.* It came to be known as the No Detention Policy.

Private schools were directed, well in advance, to ensure no students were detained. A large number of private schools were used to screening academically weak students so the school could concentrate on the good performers in order to attain a high centum in the Board examinations.

Schools responded by removing all roadblocks, the first at class X and the second, two years later, in class XII, when a central board graded the students. The students were happy there would be no more failing from now on. Their parents were happy because the children would not suffer. The teachers were happy because the scanner on them had been removed. The experts were happy because they had a provided a win-win solution. Problem solved.

And it did solve the problem in some ways. It saw a rise in enrolment and literacy, a decline in drop-outs and student anxiety and there were fewer cases of student suicides. In the beginning everybody lauded the policy and called it a success. But then the trouble started. Teachers complained that students had developed a lackadaisical attitude. Why study when there is no fear of failing? [The Hindu 14 June 2012]. There was no differentiation between the intelligent, the average and the struggling students, said teachers.

One school teacher said she was told to promote those students who had not even appeared for the final examination. Teachers like her have reason to be upset, as the same set of non-performing students, when promoted to higher classes, gave them a hard time in class. Some perform badly in Board examinations if no extra coaching is given.

The teachers were the first to sense the No Detention Policy was not in the long term interests of the students. But here again, their main concern seemed to be success vs failure. And that the non-performing students (NPS), gave them a hard time and performed badly at the Board exams. The teachers were more concerned about their own hard times, rather than those of the students. Non-performance is a dignified word for failure. The banking sector uses a similar term, Non Performing Assets or NPAs, to describe loans that have gone bad and need to be written off. It seemed that we had finally converted children into products.

From 2010, when the policy was introduced, to 2012, the number of standard 5 students unable to read even Class 2 texts increased from 46.3% to 53.2%, according to the Annual Status of Education

Report (ASER), conducted by Pratham, a respected non-profit group. The drop in math performances was even sharper. In 2010, 29.1% of standard 5 students were unable to perform simple two digit subtraction sums involving carry-overs. By 2012, this number had risen to 46.5%.

'There's a risk that we may create a generation of children who can hold up school certificates, but may not have even the most basic learning one would expect from schooling,' says Rohini Srivastava, a middle school math teacher at a secondary boys school in the national capital. Srivastava blames the 'no-failing policy' for declining attendance in her classes. 75% attendance was required for students to move to the next class before the policy was enforced. 'Now, kids know they'll get to the next class whether or not they come to school,' she says.

Child councillors are also speaking up. 'Absence of failure is not a good thing,' writes Dr Rajiv Mohta, an adolescent counsellor and paediatrician with vast experience in interacting with students, parents and teachers. 'We have now instilled in the minds of students that they are superior in every way because they cannot be failed. Students are being misled into believing they have cracked some secret code for success and are invincible. Till Std. VIII, even if they can barely spell or write, they keep passing and then suddenly, the next year, reality kicks in. Their young minds are not ready to deal with the sudden jolt and it leads to adverse effects which can scar them for life. Students take the 'invincibility' of the no-fail policy seriously and it spills into their personal life. The policy has empowered students in the wrong way. For boys, rejection by girls is a big shocker, because they have 'failed' in achieving their goal. Because of their psychological conditioning, students often take this as an insult and revenge becomes the next agenda. At home, the refusal of parents to buy them a new mobile phone, clothes etc., is not taken well. While most throw tantrums, we have seen kids even committing suicide over petty things. This no-fail policy will aggravate these issues to a great extend in the years to come. It's already showing and will certainly get worse.'

Prem Kaur, Headmistress, Government High School, Karsan, says: 'The overall system will not improve unless academic fear is implanted among students from junior classes.' Renu Puri, Principal, GMSSS, Sector 8, Chandigarh says: 'We need reforms.'

Reforms? We thought these *were* the reforms!

Let us analyze the WHO report which says 'the maximum suicides in India were committed in the age group 15-29 years'. What is troubling our youth? We have shifted the fail stops from the 6-14 age band and pushed them to later stages. Fifteen is the average age for students in class X in India. It is also the first road block, where students are tested by a Central Board. Could the suicides have something to do with the policy of replacing all the inter-lying roadblocks with one at Class X and then Class XII? Let us consider what we may have done.

One of the main issues was to reduce student stress and anxiety. We deduced they were afraid of failure. So we reacted by lowering their exposure to failure. But when they left school, they met with many road blocks – they failed to get admission to colleges, faced failure at university, in relationships, or were fired from jobs. What possibly happened was that by removing all the initial roadblocks of failure, we ended by crashing the entire system.

Youth is the time to learn. We need to make mistakes early *and* recover, under the guidance of teachers and parents. The more we push failure into adulthood, the more drastic the results. Our protectors and guides are no longer there to form our crucial support base and help recovery. As we grow up, we enter a cutthroat world, where even our friends are our competitors. Most importantly, we do not have the luxury of time to fail. At five years of age we are expected to make mistakes. At 10, we can make mistakes and amend them. At 20, the cost of failure rises exorbitantly, and at 30, failure can be a matter of life and death. Hence we need to shun our failure phobia and develop a healthy attitude towards it.

One reason for removing the failure potential in primary and secondary education was that the young were not mature enough to cope and could thus take the extreme step. But now, the legal age of adulthood is considered to be 18. There are indications that for every adult who committed suicide in the 15-29 age group, there are 20 more attempted suicides. Essentially, we have shifted all the stress from the formative years to the productive years. But in doing so we have denied the formative years of its learning and poisoned the productive years.

Pushing the failure to a later stage may have eased stress levels for some time, but it robbed students of the luxury to fail. 'If I had to live my life again, I would make the same mistakes, only sooner,' said Tallulah Bankhead, the American actress who dominated stage and screen in the 1940s. Starting early gives us time to learn.

Another interesting thing happened. The learning curve was elongated and pushed to an undefined age. This meant that children could go on making mistakes till an undefined age and the intensity of mistakes at later ages would be far greater.

Schools are all about academic conformity. There is a curriculum that everybody is taught and evaluated on. Students are declared successes or failures based on how closely they adhered to the curriculum. A student is required to attend school for 210 days in a year as per the guidelines of the Department of Education, Government of India. That means students attend school for only seven months a year. Most students, however, are not in school every day. In fact, 80% to 90% attendance is common, due to various reasons. Shaving another 10 or 20 % off 210 days leaves us with six months of school. What do students do with the other six months? For now, we will assume that six or seven months provide enough schooling to kids.

If a school works for eight hours a day, then students would be spending seven hours a day attending classes. Assuming the school follows a five-day week, student spend5x7x210 = 7350 hours every year attending classes. In the 12 years of formal schooling, a student has 7350 x12 = 88200 hours in class.

Assuming again, that he puts in another two hours a day, five days a week at home or attending private tuitions, we can safely add another 2100 hours. This makes a total of 90,300 hours of studying various subjects. This is assuming he does not study at all for 155 days (5 months), which is unlikely.

At the end of the 12 years, having spent over 90,000 hours, a child is evaluated on a single exam lasting three hours. This means three hours of evaluation for> 90,000 hours of study. He duly gets labelled F, or maybe B/C/D. That is hugely unfair. That F will stick to him for life. A grade letter worth 90,000 study hours? That is certainly expensive. Perhaps the Central Board needs to conduct evaluations at more reasonable intervals, say every 30,000 hours or every four years.

Presently students spend two years in the academic streams of their choice. A four-year evaluation would mean restructuring this pattern and devoting more time in the chosen stream, leading to more exposure and focus on the chosen subjects.

Spending more time studying chosen subjects would increase the level of interest among students, many of whom are disinterested in pursuing certain subjects and lose interest in or dropout of the schooling system. One of the most common reasons for a student not doing well is lack of interest. The feeling of being forced to study uninteresting subjects kills enthusiasm. One of the subjects most students feel challenged is Mathematics. Often these students are interested in the Humanities and Languages. They find it a relief when they are offered the choice of streams in class XI. Then there are students who wish to pursue medicine and find the advanced concepts of Trigonometry and 3 Dimensional Geometry unappealing. They wonder how and where they are going to apply those principles. It is a drain on mental resources.

Why can we not allow them to make the choice of subjects earlier? Why can we not relieve their pain and add some joy to their lives? Fourteen years is also the sentence awarded by the Indian Penal Code for heinous crimes. Are we sentencing our kids for having different interests than what is being offered? For some children school does seem like serving a prison sentence.

Kyōiku mama, is a Japanese term meaning 'education mother'. She is a 'mother who relentlessly drives her child to study, to the detriment of the child's social and physical development and emotional well-being'. The *kyōiku mama* is analogous to the American stage mother who forces her child into show-business or the Indian self-sacrificing mother who coerces her child into engineering or medical school. *Kyōiku mama* is feared by her own children, blamed by the press for school phobias and youth suicides. But Ronald Reagan praised Japan's 'one parent on the scene' who 'stays in touch with the teachers, supervises the homework, arranges extra instructional help if needed, and buttresses the child's motivation to do well in school and beyond.'

The solution, surprisingly, appears to be quite simple. All we need is to offer more choice, in different packages. Like a hotel. It is our duty to educate our children. We must make efforts to present and package education to make it interesting. We cannot say, 'Here is the food and you have to eat it'. Why lament when children leave the dishes half-eaten or untouched?

Failure at school means the dishes have been left half-eaten. And we blame the children for that, devising means of coercion and punishment to make them eat. But then we come up with a grand scheme – they are not required to finish! 'Eat as much as you want and leave the rest.' But a little later, we say, 'This is the final dish and it is mandatory to finish it.' We have only shifted the compliance bar to a later date.

But what we need to do is simply *change the dish*. Or offer more choice. There are many students who are inclined towards sports; they often form the major chunk of dropouts from school. By integrating sports as a chosen subject, we can assure willing compliance. Education by choice is far more effective than education by compulsion. Students who train for four years as sportspersons in their formative years will not only bring much needed awareness about physical fitness but sporting prowess.

There is one condition though. All subjects have to be treated on par. Sports must get as much importance as the sciences. It should not be that those unable to excel in the sciences are downgraded to sports. This equal treatment of all subjects will remove all superiority bias, which unfortunately exists among both parents and students alike. The Humanities are seen as the last refuge of weaker students. This superiority-inferiority bias has to be removed. Often, students are compelled by their parents to take up 'superior' academic streams simply to enjoy the special status the society – claiming their ward is an academic gem. The child may have no interest in such *superior* subjects. The choice of stream cannot be a prestige issue but based on the interests and abilities of the student concerned.

The fear of failure kills creativity and intelligence. The only thing it produces is conformity. But, hang on. There is something else fear promotes. Scientists have discovered that fear acts as stimulii, causing the secretion of neurotransmitters which aid memory. The mind associates the fear induced by punishment, both mental and physical, with memorizing. Could this be the reason our education system lays stress on memory recall, using methods that aid such learning?

Some things we learn on our own, such as breathing. The body mechanisms go into action as soon as we enter this world. Some things we learn by simply observing others, like walking and talking. We pick up these skills with little or no assistance. There are still other things that we need help to learn, but retain for life, like riding a bicycle or swimming. Other skill sets require special training. The things we learn on our own are retained for the longest period of time, while those we acquire under the influence of others, are more likely to be forgotten. The things we use the most, unconsciously, like walking, are retained.

Do we have the same pattern for thinking skills? Do we learn and retain some things more than others? And if we do, is it linked to the method of teaching?

2. WHY DO WE FAIL AS STUDENTS?

- Lack of interest: 'I'm not interested in this subject.'
- Lack of ability: This subject goes over my head.
- Inadequate teaching: The teacher is unable to communicate the subject matter.
- Inadequate resources at school: The school lacks basic infrastructure such as proper classrooms, blackboards, toilets and security.
- Inadequate resources at home: 'Since there is an electricity problem at home, I can't study.'
- Family issues.
- Personal and Health issues: Keep falling sick and missing classes, so unable to keep up.

3. WHO DECIDES OUR EDUCATION POLICY?

Education has always been a need based activity and its focus shifts with time. Some people at the top of the social pyramid decide 'we want this' and create a policy. In earlier times, children were trained to be soldiers or scriptural scholars. Technical knowledge was passed from clan to clan. Architects for instance, would pass on knowledge to a select few. Today, our leaders proudly declare that we must create a work force for the 21st century. But why does the state wish to build a work force? Primarily because an educated work force is easier to *control.* The educated class pays more taxes and you can even convince them that a higher tax is beneficial.

In the colonial era and a long time after that, the stress was on creating clerical staff who would help the administration run. What do clerks need to know? Language and factual data. The focus of education was thus on linguistic skills and the recalling of factual data. Students have long questioned the logic of memorizing historical dates such as, Babur fought the 1st battle of Panipat against Ibrahim Lodhi in 1526. Students are required to remember the names of the two adversaries, the battleground and the year. Why? There were no computers. In clerical work, remembering case files, laws and data, was a huge advantage as well as a requirement. This familiarity with dates tuned the mind to remember case details in government offices and courts. Instead of analysing why the invaders won the three battles of Panipat, or if Panipat was geographically a strategic location, which served as a gateway to Delhi, students limited their knowledge to chronology. Analysis was put beyond the scope of the student as the masters did not wish clerks to question their orders. The education system was designed to create an educated servant class.

Post-independence, the focus shifted to nation-building, requiring engineers and technicians. A work force was required to manufacture and build civil structures such as dams and factories. The 1990s saw the service industry gain focus. IT services, retail, banking and insurance, began to open up. These sectors demanded different skill sets again, such as data analysis, reasoning and interpretive skills.

Where do we stand today? Every student endures something of the colonial era, the industrial era, and the service sector boom. Why? Because we are afraid to let go and change. A student in middle school is smart enough to judge the relevance of what he is being taught. Once it is established that whatever is being offered is irrelevant, it becomes boring stuff and the student loses interest.

If we total the inputs of teachers, parents, private tutors, school staff and transporters, it adds up to a many man hours. For every hour, a student needs the support of at least 1 parent+1 teacher+1 school staff, therefore 90,000x3 = 270,000 hours of support. This is 30 years of support. If we take parents out, a single student generates employment for two people for 90,000/ 2x12x365 = 20 years. But let's restrict our focus to the academic front and leave the economics for later.

What is the best way to evaluate a student's 90,000 hours in school? And what of the net results?

- ☐ Did those hours result in the overall growth of the child?
- ☐ Do these hours enable him to live a healthy life?
- ☐ Does he relate positively with the society?
- ☐ Did these hours prepare him for living life as an adult?
- ☐ Do these study hours empower him to fulfil his own material requirements?
- ☐ Does he understand his responsibilities as a citizen?
- ☐ Does he believe in a harmonious co- existence with nature?
- ☐ Does this enlighten him to appreciate life?
- ☐ Does he uphold and exhibit the moral values of the society?
- ☐ Does it help him to become a person of integrity?

A school is not an information dispensing unit. It is a place where a child spends most of his formative years. It plays a major role in shaping the child and is therefore a centre of development which contributes actively towards overall personality development. The curriculum must be designed to answer the above points. A student leaving after 12 years of formal schooling should be able to evaluate and satisfy himself. A legitimate question is, what if, after an honest self-evaluation, the student finds himself falling short on any of these counts? Would it be considered a failure on the part of the school to teach or a failure of the student to learn? Would such an evaluation system work?

Success is not the key to happiness. Happiness is the key to success. If you love what you are doing, you will be successful. ~ Albert Schweitzer

Does this mean that if you do not love what you are doing, you will fail? It is assumed that happiness is the real goal. Thus, even if you 'succeed', you may not have achieved the real objective. There will be something lacking, your success will remain incomplete. Learning by rote may fetch you grades and many may call it success, but you will have missed the real purpose of learning.

If you really understand something, it will bring you happiness; you will experience the joy of learning. Grades will follow.

4. WHERE CAN POLICY HELP?

The first four issues listed earlier have to directly do with the structure of learning, guidelines for teachers and school infrastructure, as education policy. They can all be improved upon. Policy should be designed to make learning interesting.

Secondly, policy must bring about flexibility in the learning structure, accommodating students of different ability. A rigid structural approach where students of varying interests *have to* adapt is certain to cause frustration. The one-size-fits-all approach is not student-friendly and focuses on the management of education rather than the students. A student-friendly policy is needed, designed to encourage each student to continue studying, providing many choices so that the learning can be *tailored* according to his abilities and interests.

Why can't students choose to major in sports or the performing arts at school level? Why do they have to limit themselves to academic fields? Sachin Tendulkar, the cricketing legend, found it difficult to complete his education primarily because when it was exam time in India, it was cricket time somewhere in the world. He had clear priorities. He was lucky to have understanding parents who helped him make the right choice. Players who qualify for the Ranji Trophy, are often pressurized to complete university by their parents. They are forced to study subjects they have no interest in. Yet they sit for exams to fulfil the minimum requirement for higher employment - graduation.

But, for all their love of cricket, rising stars cannot afford to fail the class X Board exams (as their icon did twice), simply because they may not have the safety net of an international cricketing career.

For the other three points, we need the cooperation of society and the government on a large scale. School is a centre of structured learning, set up by society. Schools exist to teach and provide an environment for learning to happen. Schools exist for students. Without students, the school has no meaning and loses its purpose. Empty classrooms mean that students do not find them to be centres of learning anymore. Society, schools and the state, must make efforts to bring students back to classrooms. Children demand a better way to be educated. The authorities must comply, if only to justify their existence.

5. EDUCATION MARKETING: TRANSFORMING A SPIRITUAL RELATIONSHIP INTO A SERVICE PROVIDER-CONSUMER ASSOCIATION

There was a time in India when teachers were considered second only to God. It was the teacher who showed a seeker the path to God. Alas, today, a teacher has become a service provider promising results, in keeping with the market and the economy. Having lost his Godlike status, he charges a fee and service tax. The student is no longer someone in search of salvation but a consumer demanding information, value for money, and product satisfaction. The product is education. As teacher charge by the hour, students too, want results delivered at the same speed. This over-the-counter packaging of education has destroyed the sanctity and grace once associated with the process of learning. A student who once rode high on the chariot of knowledge, now questions his teacher not only to gain knowledge but also to test him, thus judging both the provider and the product. The student, as the consumer, sets the terms. He has established himself as the primary stakeholder in the education system.

6. EVALUATING THE EVALUATION SYSTEM

Our education system is evaluation-focused. We spend more time and resources in evaluating students than on educating them. On average, a middle school student studies seven subjects (English, Hindi, Maths, General Science, Social Science, Computers and a Third Language). Evaluations are done in two cycles of weekly exams and semi-annual exams. The first ensures the child is evaluated for seven weeks, while the second lasts for three weeks (including days off in-between papers). Thus, 10 weeks are used for a single evaluation cycle, becoming 20 weeks for the two cycles – from 210 school days a year. The actual recommendations of the regulatory boards require four rounds of weekly tests (formative assessments). This leaves barely two months of stress-free education. Children live in a continuous exam mode, worrying over weekly or semi-annual exams or surprise tests. The focus of education shifts from gaining knowledge to performing in exams.

Not only do students live with the constant pressure of being evaluated continuously (Comprehensive Continuous Evaluations), teachers too, remain engaged in question-answer checking, when they should be thinking of innovative ways to impart education.

The system also demands that all the students adjust to the same pace of teaching. This 'one-size-fits-all' mode of teaching is unfair as students have different learning aptitudes.

The intentions behind the CCE were to reduce student stress levels. However, it has created a system where students remain stressed throughout the academic year as one cycle of evaluations follows the other in quick succession. Not only has the system failed to reduce stress levels among students, it has increased stress levels among teachers as well. The system consumes too many resources and manpower, causing teachers and student burn-out.

There was once some incentive to learning and gaining knowledge, such as a good career which translated into material and social well-being. At some point the education system could no longer provide the necessities of a good life and the incentive for learning diminished; institutions switched to operating on fear – fear of punishment and fear of failure. Following protests from social groups, educational institutions backed down on the fear factor. Now, students have neither the incentive to learn nor the fear. After school they are disappointed not to gain from the system and disillusioned at being unequipped for what is demanded of them. Schools have been transformed from centres of learning to management centres, shifting focus to the logistics of handling children rather than on education and learning. The time and effort required to keep children disciplined and engaged, rather like a day-care centre, exceeds the time spent on real education.

7. 100 YEARS OF MCQs

MCQs have been with us for a century and have become standard evaluation formats – for the wrong reasons.That MCQs remain and thrive is not because they are the best form of evaluation, but that the format is easier, faster and cheaper for evaluators.The OMR (Optical Mark Reader) machines can evaluate over 2000 sheets in an hour, costing less than $0.10 (about 60 paise per sheet). CBSE had placed a limit of 25 answer sheets per evaluator per day. 'It is not voting that is democracy; it is counting,' commented Tom Stoppard, the British playwright. In the context of students, it is not exams which measure knowledge, but evaluation.

A BRIEF HISTORY OF MULTIPLE CHOICE QUESTIONS

1914: The American economy was booming. Immigrants were pouring in from around the world. World War I had started. The American army required huge placements but there was an issue –shortage of evaluators to assess the candidates. A quick assessment system was the need of the hour. Frederick J Kelly of State Teachers College, Kansas, took up the issue and wrote in his dissertation: 'If Henry Ford could turn out Model Ts "for the great multitude", surely there is an equivalent way to streamline schooling'. The result was the Kansas Silent Reading Test, also called 'item-response' or the 'bubble test'. It resolved two inherent problems of traditional testing – subjectivity of the teacher and the time taken to mark. Kelly provided a format wherein the question, called 'the stem', was followed by four options for the examinee to choose from (with only one right answer).

Now it was possible for anyone to administer an evaluation without being conversant with the subject. All that was needed was the right scoring key to the test. Thus there was no need for evaluators to be teachers as well. It was also faster, since only the scoring key had to be matched. The important point was that MCQs were designed with the objective of solving a management issue. And this is the sole reason this evaluation tool has survived and thrived over a hundred years, with most institutions adopting it as a default mechanism.

But the problem with objective type questions is that they are just that – objective. One is either right or wrong. There is no merit in partial knowledge. If one understands the principle but makes a mistake in answering, one gets no credit. But if one does not know the answer at all, one can still pass by playing on probability or making an intelligent guess. Is it then a true measure of knowledge? I have serious doubts.

8. LOTS (Lower Order Thinking Skills) VS HOTS (Higher Order Thinking Skills)

Bloom's Taxanomy shows the LOTS which form the essential base for the learning pyramid and the HOTS developing as we move towards the top. Lower Order does not mean that they are non-essential or trivial. Rather the Lower Order is the foundation on which the Higher Order develops.

LOTS

- Memorize
- Recall
- Understand

HOTS

- Analyse different perspectives
- Associate partswith whole
- Classify
- Comparing and contrasting
- Evaluating
- Explain cause and effect
- Generate possibilities
- Identify and Explain patterns
- Inferring
- Association -Makingconnections
- Predict
- Problem solving
- Sequencing
- Synthesizing
- Uncovering motives

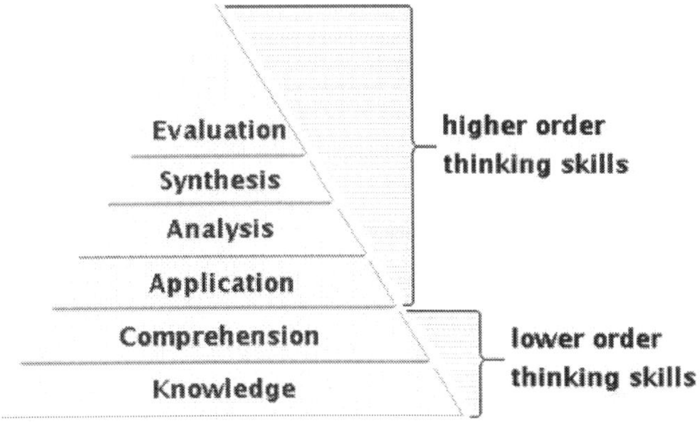

There is yet another issue with MCQs. They were designed primarily to measure LOTS. Kelly based his thesis on students of grades VI-VIII, while the US Army used it for entry-level cadets with little education. MCQs were never meant for mass evaluation at higher levels. But the ease of evaluation, economic viability and quick results, has elevated its acceptance at all levels of knowledge evaluation. Today, MCQs are standard from early schooling to post-graduate, technical tests. The Government uses the format for recruitments into the prestigious Civil and Defence Services as well as a host of other public services.

WHAT MCQs DON'T MEASURE

For one, MCQs don't measure possibilities. What if the question offers other possible answers than those listed? There is no credit for unnecessary thinking. MCQs are not the right tool to assess most HOTS. They eliminate presentation skills and coherence of ideas, both of which are considered essential in many disciplines. Questions need to be framed in a manner that allows us to think beyond the MCQ answers.

Here is a simple example: How many senses do we have? The usual answer: Touch, hearing, taste, smell and sight. But how would students respond if we framed the question in an open-ended manner? How many senses can you think of besides touch, hearing, taste, smell and sight? (No, it is not a trick question. Nor is the answer in the realm of the extra sensory). Some would no doubt leave the question unanswered, some would think of wild things, but a few would come up with sensible answers. Here are a few starters to fire your mind.

- Sense of balance (vestibular sense): Perhaps the most important sense, without which we would not be able to walk properly. It is related to a specific organ – the three semi-circular canals in the internal ear. This sense causes motion sickness, vomiting and nausea.
- Sense of Temperature (thermoception): You can feel how hot or cold a room is by just stepping outside, without ever touching anything.
- Sense of Pressure: Experienced underwater or during air travel.
- Sense of Pain: Our skin perceives pain. But what of internal pain, when we have a muscle tear, a fracture, a stomach ache or a splitting headache?

There are a host of other senses that we use without being conscious of them. Like catching a ball by positioning our hands underneath it, knowing when to pee or stop eating. Physiologists have identified as many as 27 different senses. So why stop at five? The answer lies in ancient Greece. The concept of five senses hasn't been updated since then. Indians, however, have long identified the Mind as the sixth sense.

Training the mind with open-ended questions allows us to explore beyond the limits of what has been taught. This, of course, requires the teacher to be as imaginative as the students, in order to appreciate their responses. But a complete overhaul of the present system would prove both overwhelming and unmanageable. But an introduction of the above process would be a good step forward.

Here is another. Which is the most dangerous subject? 'It all depends what you mean by 'dangerous', you may reply. Let us clarify 'dangerous' to mean in the context of society. I am pretty certain the answers would relate to war. But consider this –literature has the power to influence and shape the minds of individuals, communities and nations into believing both good and bad. Literature can motivate a person to blow himself up in an act of war – because s/he believes. Only when the deed is done do others perhaps realise it was wrong.

9. CASE STUDY: INDIAN VS HONG KONG VS SINGAPORE EDUCATION SYSTEM MODEL

India and Hong Kong share a common reality – both were British colonies. While India gained independence in 1947, Hong Kong shed colonialism only 50 years later, in 1997, when it was handed back to China. But there is another similarity. Both have the British education system as a legacy. Both have made changes. Like most nations, India and Hong Kong provide for 12 years of formal education. India follows a 10+2+3 model, while HK has a 3+3+4 system called the 334 scheme. The Singapore model is the most interesting, and is the basis for the ideas suggested in this book.

THE INDIAN SYSTEM

Nursery +KG	I to V	VI to X	XI & XII	IyIIyIIIy
Age: 3- 4	5 - 9	10 - 14	15 - 16	17-19
Pre-Primary	Primary	Secondary	Sr. Secondary	University
				2 core +3 elective

THE HONG-KONG SYSTEM: K 334

Nursery+KG	Forms 1 - 3	Forms 3 - 55	I- VI	Iy - Vy
Age: 3 -4	5 - 10	11 - 13,	14 - 16,	17 - 20,
	Jun Secondary	4 core +3 elective	Sen Secondary	

Secondary education consists of 3 + 3 + 4 (three years of junior secondary, followed by three years of senior secondary then 4 years of university). The first year of secondary school, known as Form or Secondary One, follows six years of primary education. Forms 1–3 have compulsory attendance and in junior secondary, the learning is broader, without students choosing specific study areas.

Students in Forms 4-6 prepare for the HKDSE, the examinations held at the end of Form 6. There are four core subjects – English, Mathematics, Chinese and Liberal Studies. Students then choose two or three elective subjects from 20 offered. There are also applied learning subjects modelled on the idea of BTEC. Six modern foreign languages also form part of the students' choices. The main difference with the Indian system is starting the electives a year earlier and a four-year university programme.

THE SINGAPORE SYSTEM

Primary education in Singapore normally starts at age seven. It is a four-year *foundation stage* (Primary 1-4), and a two-year *orientation stage*. *Foundation* is the first stage of formal schooling. All pupils advance to the orientation stage after Primary 4, when they follow streams according the pupil's ability, known as 'subject-based banding'. Students study subjects at different levels based on their scores in various subjects at the end of Primary 4. After six years of Primary education, students sit for the national Primary School Leaving Examination (PSLE). They then choose the secondary school of their choice, based on their results in this examination. They are assigned to a secondary school based on merit and choice. Based on results of the PSLE, students are placed in various secondary education streams: Special, Express, Normal (Academic), and Normal (Technical).

On completion of secondary school, students (apart from IB), take the Singaporean GCE O Level – the results of which determine which pre-universities or post-secondary institutions they can apply to. Pre-university includes junior colleges offering two-year courses leading up to the GCE A Level, and the Millennia Institute, which offers a three-year course leading to the GCE 'A' Level. They all accept students on merit, with a greater emphasis on academics than on vocational technical education. Students who wish to pursue vocational education, go to polytechnics or the Institute of Technical Education (ITE), where they receive a diploma upon successful completion of the chosen course.

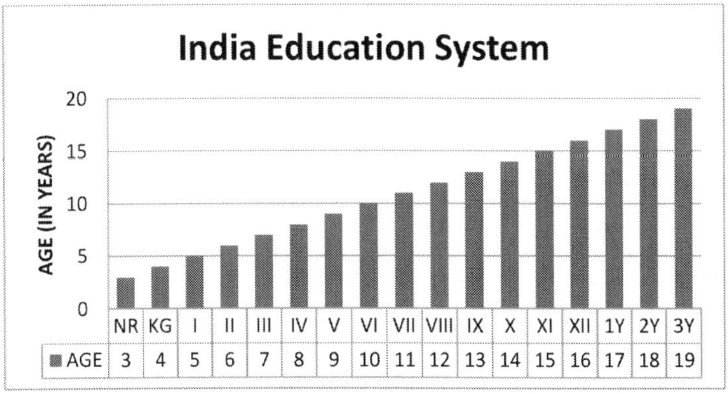

	NR	KG	I	II	III	IV	V	VI	VII	VIII	IX	X	XI	XII	1Y	2Y	3Y
AGE	3	4	5	6	7	8	9	10	11	12	13	14	15	16	17	18	19

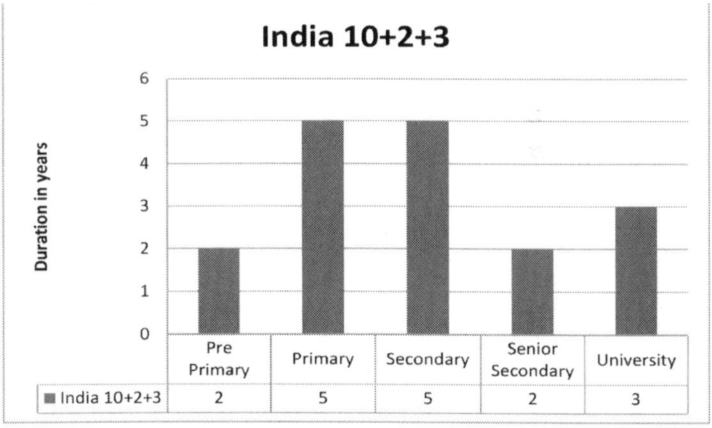

	Pre Primary	Primary	Secondary	Senior Secondary	University
India 10+2+3	2	5	5	2	3

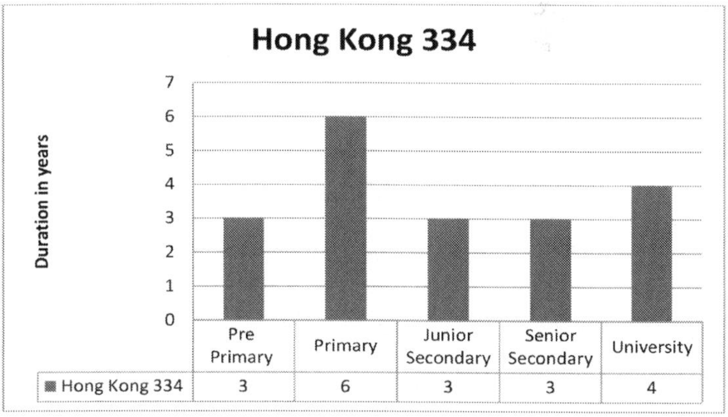

	Pre Primary	Primary	Junior Secondary	Senior Secondary	University
Hong Kong 334	3	6	3	3	4

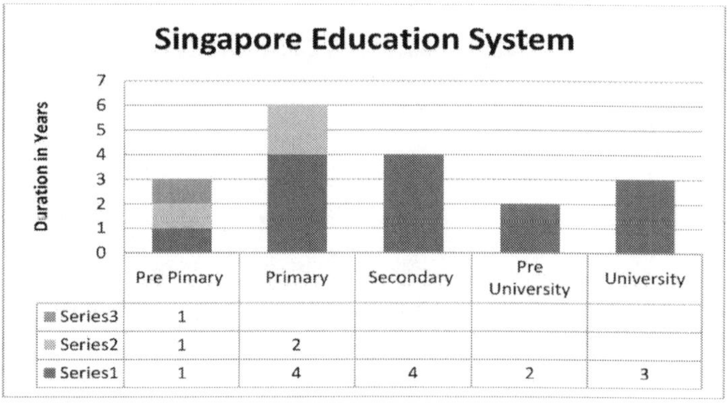

10. FAILING BY CHOICE: FAILURE OF THE VALUE SYSTEM

We are living in a situation where teachers do not want to teach, and students do not want to study. Patients are suing doctors, while doctors are charging exorbitant fees for being noble. The lawyers are joining hands with rivals and misguiding their own clients. The police and mafia are difficult to distinguish. The true rouges have become our leaders. Journalists have turned into media planners for the rich and powerful, controlling and manufacturing news to serve their pipers. It is difficult to determine who has succeeded and who has failed, for what reason.

Though it may seem so, this is not a cynical view of what's happening around us. It is realistic. While everyone is not as portrayed above, the trend is clear and strong. But why do we need to discuss it here? One of the meanings of failure is: Failing to perform a duty or expected action. We discuss failure at the individual level but overlook that the society, *collectively*, is failing. People do not do what they are supposed to do; they have become untrue to their professions. *They have chosen to fail.* A student may decide that whatever is being taught does not conform to the real world and hence makes a choice to fail.

The question which arises is: Why are we making this conscious choice to fail? Can it be that we are not failing but *changing* to adapt to a newer value system? Let's understand that this chaos is not a bomb that exploded suddenly. It is a change that occurred steadily, causing value systems to fail. Where does this failure begin?

There is a clear disconnect between what is being taught in school and what exists in society – how we want others to behave as well as how we behave. What we wish to see is what we teach in school; outside, we do what we have to get things done. Inside school there exists the idea of an ideal society, upholding ethics and values we hold dear and *hope* to follow. But when a child steps into the real world, he finds that what he has learnt does not map out. There seem to be two worlds, run by different rules.

Today we are dealing with smart kids. Gen-next is more informed and sensitive to the changes happening in society. They are aware of the disconnect between the idealism of school and the realism of life. One of the reasons they fail is because they find the educational system irrelevant. The kids we label as failures or underperformers are actually intelligent enough to see the futility of pursuing such a system. They *choose* to fail. This is the reason why some students who do not do well in school, excel in the real world, while some who excel in school are shocked when they leave that ideal world.

What can we do and how? The first question is: Do we *need* to correct this imbalance between idealism in school and realism in society? The answer is a big Yes! And urgently.

There are three ways to correct the imbalance.

1. By tuning the 'ideal' system in school to a more realistic level prevailing in society. This would involve exposing children to the dirty tricks people play, rather like vaccinating them in order to develop resistance to reality.
2. By changing the 'realism' of the outside world to idealism, by correcting major discrepancies.
3. Creating a mix of idealism and realism and so making education relevant; shifting focus from factual or Google learning, which involves memorizing facts, to developing interpretive skills and decreasing mandatory subjects while providing more options to choose from.

To raise the level of education we must first raise the level of educators. Traditionally medicine and teaching were considered equally noble professions. Today, the status of teachers needs to be elevated to match doctors, making teaching a top career option.

There is a saying, 'Those who can, do. Those who cannot, teach.' Teaching is never considered the first choice for doers. But when all else fails, teaching becomes the default choice. We must reverse this trend and bring in people whose dream job is to teach and build societies. For this there have to be incentives in the form of status and remuneration so the best candidates, with passion, join as faculty. At present those who join this noble profession find their friends, or even students, raking in money while they barely survive the blows of inflation.

There are many things that policy-makers can do to help, such as increasing teacher salaries, making it tax free (we provide tax free status to farmers who feed us, so why not teachers, who are playing a vital role in nation-building?) We can also provide teachers with special privileges in public services such as railways, airways and local transport. Most teachers give private tuitions to make ends meet. A non-teaching allowance on the lines of a non-practicing allowance for doctors can be considered. While this is the domain of policy makers, many suggestions are available from the people they are put in office to serve.

The next step is to choose the right role models. Society must choose carefully as role models are accorded the status of examples to the people around them. We often honour the rich, even when we know they have accumulated their wealth by unfair means. By making real estate agents and stock brokers role models, we cannot expect our children to attain the Nobel Prize.

PART III: THE FAILURE FACTOR

And why do we fall, Bruce? So we can learn to pick ourselves up.
Batman

1. FAILURE AS ENTRY FEE TO THE THEATRE OF SUCCESS

Consider this list: Abraham Lincoln, Amitabh Bachchan, Rabindranath Tagore, Dr. Abdul Kalam, Michael Jordan, Walt Disney, Henry Ford, The Beatles, Bill Gates, Paul Allen, Stephen King, J.K. Rowling. What is common to all the names? They are all A-listers in their professions. *So what makes them stand out?*

They all suffered devastating bouts of failure in their lives. Some were even called 'failures with no future' from childhood. And the list does not end there; rather it is just the beginning. There are hundreds of authors whose works were rejected by numerous publishers before they were accepted and went on to become all-time bestsellers. There are great inventors who were labelled 'mad scientists' creating impossible projects. There are singers, actors and musicians who have been told they were wasting their time. But they did not do something else, and went on to become celebrities in their fields.

But could it be that failure played a positive role in their lives and provided them with the necessary resolve to become outliers? These remarkable people succeeded despite failures, with the odds stacked against them? Could it be these illustrious people succeeded not despite but *because* of their failures?

I can sense some objections - the primary one being that we are indulging in statistical cherry picking. For every Michael Jordan, there are thousands who were equally dedicated to the sport but got nowhere. For every J.K. Rowling there are many, many authors who fall by the wayside, failing to be published, let alone make it to any bestseller list. The world is full of people who have received a rather generous dose of failure and they honestly believe failure has done them no good. We shall certainly address this point but first, let's see if the thesis has any value.

2. THE MANY FACES OF FAILURE

Failure is anything we attempt which does not yield expected results. We struggle with failures every day, encountering it in different avatars: Failure to get up in time to catch the school bus; failure to keep up with the morning walk; failure to hit the ball in a cricket match; failure to get good marks in school. As we grow up the avenues of failure increase: Entrance exams, college admissions, job prospects, marriage etc. Our nasty friend is always lurking close by. Failure has the power to deeply affect your behaviour. It can cause worry or totally destroy you.

3. THE DARK SIDE OF FAILURE

The realization that you have failed is the most depressing and devastating side of failure. It hits you smack in the face and shakes you up, causing deep hurt. The darker side is the shattering of your dreams, leaving you to face bitter reality. In the darkest hours of our tryst with failure, the mind is overcast by the impossibility of achieving success. We doubt our own capabilities. This is the moment when we vow to return to accepted ways and shun any innovative thoughts that have been bubbling in the mind. It is time to kill all risk as we mourn the death of our drive.

But is failure really the end of the world? Is there perhaps a better life after the fall? When we are unsure of ourselves and need guidance, we seek out those who have succeeded. We believe they have a formula for success. We never think of consulting those who have failed, yet they are often the ones who can point out possible minefields and pitfalls from their own experience.

Indian mythology has a rich collection of stories where obstacles are created to test individuals. Kings are tested to see whether they are worthy to rule, seekers are tested to see if they are ready to receive knowledge, and women are tested for chastity. These tests are designed to make the person fail.

One famous example is King Harish Chandra, a just king. One day, sage Vishwamitra paid him a visit. Harish Chandra honoured him by requesting the sage to ask for anything. Vishwamitra asked for his kingdom. The king obliged and departed with his wife and son. Thereafter, the sage added a twist in the tale and asked for *dakshina* (payment given to a teacher). To obtain the money, Harish Chandra sold his wife, and then himself to a *chandaal* (one who performs the last rites at the cremation ground). Meanwhile, his son was bitten by a snake and died. When the body of the boy was brought for cremation, the king wept, but duty bound, asked his wife for the cremation fees. The queen did not have any money so Harish Chandra suggested she pay for their son's last rites by cutting cloth from her clothing. Just as she was about to do so, Vishwamitra appeared on the scene to inform them it had been done as a test of the king's righteousness. The dead prince awoke as if from a deep sleep and Harish Chandra was re-installed as king. The story has been told for centuries in India to inculcate values and a sense of duty.

There is, however, another view. The sage wished to test the king and so introduced failure into the king's life. With each failure, his values were tested to breaking point. It can be said that he failed as a king by handing over the kingdom to a sage who knew nothing of governance; he failed as husband when he auctioned his wife; and then as a father when he asked for the fee for performing the last rites for his own son. And yet he stood by his beliefs about righteousness (how many would agree?), and thus claimed greatness. So was King Harish Chandra great or did his failures spurred him to attain greatness?

In a world where everyone is mad about chasing success, why would anyone *seek to fail*? But can we use failure to our advantage? Failure defines our limits, which need to be breached.

Everybody falls the first time. ~ The Matrix

Neo has mastered Jujitsu, the martial art form, in a matter of seconds. He has given a tough fight to Morpheus and begun to believe in himself. Everyone in Nebuchadnezzar was watching. Awestruck.

Morpheus asked the JUMP Programme to be loaded.

Taking a leap of faith, Neo attempts to jump and falls. The eagerly watching crew of the ship feels let down.

Mouse: Wha...what does this mean?

Switch: It doesn't mean anything...

Cypher: Everybody falls the first time. Right, Trin?

Falling or Failing may not mean anything. Everyone, even the greatest of our heroes fail. There is no need to pass judgements on every falling especially if it is the first time.

Even *The One* can fail. Even He has his own learning cycle to complete and failures to suffer before he achieves perfection.

Falling or failing may not mean anything. Everyone, even the greatest of our heroes, fail. There is no need to pass judgement on every failure, especially the first time. If I can comfortably run one kilometre and give up because I don't feel like going on, one kilometre becomes my fail point. I could continue running in that comfort zone, with a one kilometre limit and achieve 100% success. Or I could *seek to fail* by trying to break that limit.

Failure is an uncomfortable state but it can also be an exhilarating experience. When a child stumbles and falls while taking his first steps, do we label him a failure? On the contrary, the parents marvel and express their jubilation. They encourage him to get up and try again, knowing he may fall again. Are they then pushing their child towards failure? On the contrary, they believe the child has broken out of his comfort zone of crawling and reached his fail-point. In other words, he has overcome his fear of failure. So they encourage him to try again.

(If a=b, b=c then it follows that a=c)

Failure = Taking Risks; Taking Risks = Success;

Then Failure = Success

When was the last time you celebrated your failure?

'Expect that a quarter of your projects will fail. If not, you are not risking enough,' says Adam Smith, Co-founder of tech start-up Xobini. "Companies that don't embrace failure and continue to experiment eventually get in the desperate position where the only thing they can do is make a Hail Mary bet at the end of their corporate existence,' says Jeff Bezoes, Founder-CEO of Amazon.

com, explaining the many failures, worth billions of dollars, that he has had.

4. FAILURE = VACCINE OF SUCCESS

Why do we fail? We blame it on many things, ranging from bad luck to the cosmos conspiring against us. But there are some who believe that small doses of failure work like vaccines to boost the success causing changes in our mentality.

We do not do a lot of things because of the *fear* of failing. We invent reasons to postpone meetings, procrastinate about important decisions, simply to run away from the fear of failure lurking somewhere in our minds. It is also true that sometimes we actually *do* certain things because of fear. Failure and fear of it becomes the driving force

So is failure all bad? Probably not. We need to accept failure in small doses so we can be free of its debilitating effects. While we do not plan to fail, perhaps there are cases when we *do* introduce failure into the lives of our dear ones, in small doses, to prepare them to deal with greater challenges. Unbelievable? Yes, but true.

This is not to say that we plan our activities to fail or push a baby to sprint. That would be against the human ethos and result in chaos. What *is* being suggested is that if we introduce small amounts of failure, in a controlled manner, so that we induce the body and mind into unlocking their huge potential. Recipients of these small doses of failure can be taught to analyze and learn from their experiences. We know failure can be an excellent teacher, far more effective than success, but only if we are willing to learn. By learning from failure we can prepare to react to failure. It is part of a process and needs to be accepted accordingly. There is no need to fear failure. Anybody can fail. There is no reason to be depressed; look for ways to improve.

5. INSIGHTS FROM THE GAME OF CHESS

Why do we fail? There are many reasons but all of them can be brought down to just three:

1. We stopped paying attention.
2. We failed to consider all possible strategies for winning and gave up.
3. We planned our positions based on the assumed reactions of others. When they reacted differently, our plans failed.

These lessons I learned from playing chess and they have held true in real life situations as well. We do not always make a move to win. At times we know our piece faces danger and will be taken, yet we look the other way. At other times, we deliberately make a move to put our piece in danger, expecting the opponent to react by taking it. Assuming he does, we plan more moves. But sometimes the opponent has a plan of his own and behaves differently.

Chess is a mind game played between two people. If you know the character of your opponent, his fears, passions and temperament, you start the game with a definite advantage. The idea is to engage your opponent in a fake warfare so that his focus is diverted and he uses up his resources. At the same time the real war is being played in a different corner.

The first reason we fail is because we stop looking and lower our guard. We lose touch with reality. We become so engrossed with strategy that we stop paying attention to what the opponent is doing as he quietly builds his position strategically. And then, while we are on a high and about to go in for the kill, he strikes and all is lost. Another situation in which we lower our guard is when we cannot face any more attacks.

It is said that politics is the art of the possible, meaning anything can change at any point. There are no permanent friends or enemies. Chess is the art of strategies. There are so many and new possibilities become active at every stage. Choosing the right strategy becomes difficult.

In games such as cricket, the ball or bat appears to have a mind of its own. The ball may nick the bat when, in fact, the batsman wanted to hit the ball flush. The batsman may get lucky and the ball could go for a six, or land in the hands of a fielder. In soccer, the ball may hit the goal post; hitting the outer edge will take it into the crowds while the inner edge will net it. Lucky or unlucky?

In chess there is no concept of luck. There are only omissions and mistakes. The only luck involved is if the other player does not turn up or cannot complete the match. The pieces don't have minds of their own. Yet, we still hope to get lucky, that the opponent will fall for our ploys and commit mistakes. And we actually *assume=* he has. This is our undoing for while the chess pieces may not have minds of their own, the opponent certainly has.

6. THE CHINESE GROWTH STORY

In 1978, the Chinese leader, Deng Xiaoping, visited New Delhi. He marvelled at the robust growth he saw around him and commented that India was way ahead of China in terms of economic growth. Four years later, India hosted the Asian Games.

China, in 1978, was an economic failure. There was chaos and political turmoil. For the next 20 years, one heard little from China. Then suddenly, everyone began taking note of its economy. The Chinese Dragon had awoken. By 2004, the Dragon had become the growth engine of world economy. In 2008, China hosted the Olympics in Beijing, showcasing its development. What transpired in those 20 years? What magic did Deng Xiaoping perform?

The Chinese were just following the bamboo growth pattern. In those 20 years, Deng decided to bring world trade to China. They passed regulations for a Special Economy Zones in Shenzhen, Zhuhai, Shantou in Guangdong Province, and Xiamen in Fujian Province, while designating the whole of Hainan as a special economic zone. In 1984, 14 coastal cities were opened up to overseas investment.

What did these SEZs do? These were huge regions with special focus on exports. They had special tax incentives to invite foreign capital. But more than that, the regions were provided the necessary infrastructure to support manufacturing activity. In the 20 years when no one heard from China, they quietly built highways, mega factories, increased capacities for power generation, developed ports and airports, and world class hotels. In short, they did what the tiny bamboo shoot did for four years: built support for forthcoming growth. Once the infrastructure was in place, factories producing and ports busy, we heard the BOOM. Like the bamboo shooting up 80 feet in one year.

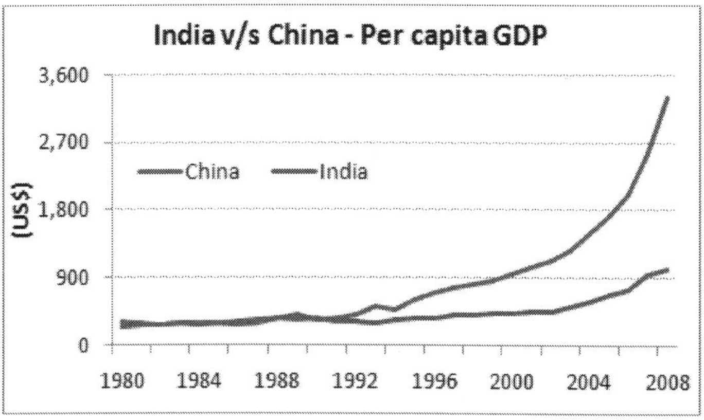

In 2010, India managed to host the Commonwealth Games but even today, we do not have the capacity to hold the Olympics. The tortoise can actually win the race. In 1978, India's GDP was 139 billion US dollars, while China was at 216 billion USD. This meant India's per capita income was higher than China's, given the higher population. But by 2008, the figures had changed dramatically in favour of the Chinese. While India progressed on the population front, she fell behind economically.

7. NOTHING FAILS LIKE SUCCESS: WHY ENTREPRENEURS FAIL

Lessons In Failure From Venture Capitalists

Identifying risks is part of the venture capital business. Money is invested to support entrepreneurial ventures believing their vision and projections of profits. But even the most successful venture capitalists follow a rule of thumb: 40% of investments will fail, 40% will produce a moderate return, and 20% a high return.

Entrepreneurs flirt with risk, which sometimes overwhelms them. Venture capitalists too, are not risk averse but they need to know where they stand and take the necessary precautions. Bill & Susan Richardson and Sonny Nwankwo came out with their *Frog* classification, indicating reasons why entrepreneurs fail, dividing them into four classes.

1 *The Boiled Frog Entrepreneur*: It is said that when a frog is dropped into boiling water it immediately leaps out, sensing the heat. But when the frog is placed in cold water, which is slowly heated, the frog remains there and is boiled. The boiled frog symbolizes the entrepreneur who fails to understand the changes happening around him. He fails to appreciate changes in consumer needs, technology upgrades or the competition. He continues to play by the same rules, complacent with his initial successes, and is gradually rendered obsolete.

2 *The Drowned Frog Entrepreneur*: After initial successes, many entrepreneurs develop an urgent need to expand and be present in every corner of the market. They take on huge debts and show a lot of promise, but eventually drown in their own expansion plans. The fact is they lack the manpower and technical know-how required for expansion. This phenomenon was common during the retail boom in India, when chains invested heavily in real estate to set up stores, accumulating huge debts. The companies had planned to sell their holdings to foreign companies. The Government failed to pass legislation allowing foreign investment in the retail sector. The companies were left with unmanageable real estate and unpayable debts.

3. *The Bullfrog Entrepreneur*: This is the classic case of success going to the head. Initial success makes them splurge recklessly on a personal level, placing themselves before the business. This was common in the dot com boom of 2000, as a new generation kids suddenly came into big money and spent lavishly, billing it as business expenses.

4. *The Tadpole Entrepreneur*: Many entrepreneurial ventures are like tadpoles. They show excellent growth in the initial phase and show potential but fizzle out just as quickly. They never grow up, but remain tadpoles for the rest of their life cycle.

8. THE MEASURE OF SUCCESS (OR FAILURE)

How do you measure a person's success? How do you grade on a five-point system, whether someone has attained great success or couldn't get off the starting line?

- ☐ Fame
- ☐ Power
- ☐ Wealth
- ☐ Knowledge
- ☐ Influence on people

The answer is very subjective. Would you consider Al Capone successful? Notorious? Without getting technical, he certainly scores well on all five success parameters. Why have some celebrities, on the right side of the law, with all their success, fame and fortune, declared themselves as failures and tried to end their own lives? Sometimes good people make bad choices and the result reflects as failure. That does not mean they are bad people. Similarly, bad people can make good choices and succeed. Branding people as failures or winners on the basis of their choice is a major reason for the erosion of values in our society.

We rarely talk of enthusiasm or happiness as parameters of success. But without them, success is meaningless. Success has different definitions in the changing phases of our life. In the initial years, work is the medium to achieve fame, power, wealth or knowledge. At some point, however, work itself becomes the best perk. The opportunity to continue working becomes the driving force, especially when we are past our prime, often becoming necessary to sustain life. So can we claim that work, the opportunity and ability to do it, becomes equated with success?

We know fame and power are temporary. We know wealth can be lost. Knowledge is based on understanding which can become outdated. It is far more difficult to make people listen, let alone influence them. And yet, knowing the temporary nature of these faces of success, we are still willing to do anything; adopt any means, fair or foul, to achieve success.

Failure = Practice
Failure = Learning
Failure = Experience
Failure = Progress
Failure = Growth
Failure ➔ Success

PART IV: THE ANATOMY OF FAILURE

1. WHY DOES FAILURE HURT?

Any talk on failure ultimately turns to a discussion on success. It is bound to, simply because that is the real objective. While success brings euphoria, failure clouds the mind in dejection. This depressive condition can either put us into a state of paralysis, where any action is prevented by fear of failure, self-doubt and lack of will, or it can lead to us doing negative things to ourselves or society.

The objective of this work is to view failure as a part of success. Success itself is not an event. Rather, it is the *result* of a series of events. Failure is simply one of those events. A failure simply means something has not worked in the manner we intended. We missed something and need to rectify it and move on. That's all.

Why does failure cause pain?

- The stakes may be high; accepting losing big is difficult.
- It was the chance of a lifetime. We think there may not be another chance.
- We may have already factored in a win.

- We often believe a win is certain and base our future planning on that assumption. Failure in such a case crashes our plans like a tower of cards. We may have already sold our chickens when the crash comes.
- We have not identified the risk factors and situations where a win may not happen.
- A sudden failure causes more pain than something for which we are prepared (ie: a 50:50 chance). We assume a win but never a loss. Being optimistic does not mean overlooking risk factors.

Failure = Not Trying. The opposite of success is not failure. It is *not trying*.

2. REDEFINING FAILURE

Success is 99% failure. ~ Soichiro Honda.

When a desired result is not achieved, we term it a failure. I believe we need to re-define it. When we attempt to solve an issue and fail, we are generating an important input to the solution. We may need to apply different methods and techniques; some may not work, or possible none. It may be necessary to think quite differently to achieve the solution. Science is based on experiments, a huge percentage of which yield results that cannot be called successes. Edison conducted tens of thousands of experiments before achieving success with his light bulb. He said: 'I have not failed. I've just found 10,000 ways that won't work.' Failure should thus be defined as an act of inaction – not taking action because of the fear of failing.

> Evaluating the causes of failure allows us to map the path to success. Each step must be executed successfully to achieve the final result. By not trying we eliminate all possibilities of success. Rather than getting undesirable results, *not trying* is the real definition of failure.

3. ALGORITHM OF SUCCESS

1. try
2. fail
3. evaluate
4. try again

Not to fail ≠ Success. Not failing does not imply a definite success. It can mean a stalemate. It can mean nobody won, or it can simply mean the decision is still pending and results are not out yet.

4. PAIN OF REGRET VS PAIN OF FAILURE

The pain of failure is undoubtedly severe but it also yields an important by-product – experience. This valuable knowledge guides our next steps in problem-solving. Failure tells us what not to repeat. The lingering pain of failure is a reminder we did not perform well, so we need to review and change our approach. Perhaps we haven't understood the problem at all. It forces us to acknowledge that something is wrong in our approach. It forces us to change our perspective or methodology, or both.

The pain of regret brings initial relief as we withdraw into the safe zone of inaction. We convince ourselves the job was not worth attempting and was bound to fail. So we rejoice. The pain of regret starts at a later stage, when the excitement of being 'saved' is over and we begin to ponder the lost opportunity, what could have happened and how differently we could have reacted. So next time, when opportunity knocks, we are faced with the same dilemma – should we act (facing the possibility of failure) or retreat into the safe zone? It is like a person waiting on a river bank, waiting to jump in or not. The only people immune to the pain of regret are the faithful believers of Murphy's Law: If anything can go wrong, it will. So why bother attempting anything?

Failure ≠ the Opposite of Success
Failure ≠ the End of the World

5. WHO IS AFRAID OF REJECTION?

We hate to admit it, but we all are. Fear of being rejected isn't just another version of the fear of failure, although it is often difficult to distinguish between the two. The fact is that fear of rejection has grown into its own space. Rejection is known to cause mental hurt that is as great, if not more, than physical pain. How? Whenever we suffer a physical injury, certain areas of the brain get activated, sending chemicals to deal with the situation. In case of rejection, scientists found through MRI scans that the *same* areas respond. Even the chemicals thrown into the blood stream are the same. What does this tell us about the character of rejection?

1. Rejection is on par with physical pain. It can be as bad as a swollen arm, a wound or a fractured bone.
2. Like all pain-causing events, we learn to avoid it. We take precautions while walking on the road or climbing stairs; we know we will get hurt if we don't. So we train our brains to keep off dangerous activities. In the same way, our minds anticipate situations which may result in rejection, and we try to stop them from happening.

What makes rejection a life-threatening danger? Anthropologists trace the fear of rejection to our primal past, to when man was a hunter. Hunting was dangerous. Living alone in conditions where anything could go wrong invoked fear of the unknown. Living together was a survival requirement and the fear of being ex-communicated (a real threat to life), manifested as the fear of rejection. In the modern world rejection comes in many guises – friendship, love, college admissions, job interviews, marriage and business proposals (and, of course, book proposals). The sense of belonging to a group, pleasing parents at home, teachers at school, friends in the playground, and the boss at office, are all instances of craving for conformity. And acceptance.

Do not get bogged down by rejection and give up on what you may be doing. But at the same time you need to understand that people are not obliged to accept whatever you are proposing. They may have valid reasons or not; worse, they may not even bother to let you know, as is common (almost a norm), in the publishing industry, where authors keep submitting their work *hoping* to get a response, even a rejection. Most wait endlessly with hope dying a slow death. Almost every new author, actor, singer or performer goes through this rejection process. It is like a rite of passage, an endurance test that must be faced.

The same is true for job openings, where hundreds of applications are received for a few positions. Most will be rejected simply because there just aren't enough openings. This does not mean that all those rejected have been pronounced as failures. Don't kill yourself just yet, there is life after rejection.

Rejection, like failure, is a test of passion. Every rejection is an opportunity to improve and steel your resolve. But it is also time for a reality check. Rethink and ask yourself: 'Do I really want this?' If the answer is still 'yes', don't look back. Remember, the first rejection causes the most hurt. But the mind toughens.

Rejection has a few hidden virtues. It exposes us to an important element of success: humility. An element that is, unfortunately, learned the hard way. The best teacher of humility is that slap in the face. Surviving rejection opens us to seeking help from anywhere, and burying our pride. A few rejections are good, even necessary, but many can be a real, long-term pain like a wound that never heals.

How bad can the wound of rejection be? It often leaves deep scars, reminding us of negative incidents (which may have occurred decades ago). The pain of rejection, unlike physical injury, does not go away. Rejection affects an individual's perception and behaviour.

It can adversely affect his emotional and psychological health. At the extreme end, it can prove fatal. The newspapers are full of reports of kids, unable to bear the pain of rejection, deciding to end their lives.

Reacting to rejection by becoming a rebel can be even more dangerous, as the person may vent his anger on society. In either of these extreme cases, the psyche of the person is under tremendous pressure as he struggles with emotional trauma. Unfortunately, the effects of rejection are not limited to individuals. Ganging up of bullies can take a serious turn and affects communities and nations. These groups often live with scarred mental states. Their anger explodes as violence as *they* reject their rejecters.

6. GOALS VS ASPIRATION

We often mistake goals with aspirations, using the terms interchangeably when, in fact, goals are intermediate stages to reach our aspirations. Aspirations are big; goals are smaller We need to pass through a series of goals to reach our aspirations.

Suppose you aspire to serve as a medical doctor. You divide the journey by breaking it into goals or stages such as moving through primary-middle–secondary and then higher secondary school education. Then your second goal is to sit for the entrance exams. The next goal is to complete the years of medical school. Goals are specific, reachable and incrementally challenging.

We often say that a goal is reached, but actually a goal needs to be *breached*. Life does not stop at the goal; we have to move past it. In soccer, the ball has to go past the goal line. The net and bars are there to simply define the goal. But in life, what if we fail to reach or breach it? We need to think of an alternate path to go around it. Or maybe move the goal posts a bit, redefining the intermediates stages to our aspirations and adjusting to circumstances.

What if you cannot get past the medical entrance stage? Then comes the test of your resolve. Are you prepared to serve *only* as a doctor or are you willing to explore other ways? You need to confirm your basic aspiration. Was the primary objective to serve or were you perhaps drawn to respect doctors receive in society? Failure gives you an opportunity to rethink your own motivations.

When we mix goals with aspirations and stumble at an intermediate stage, we often think it is the end. 'That's it. I've failed and this is the end of my dream.' All we see is the end of the road and this tunnel vision makes failure bigger and more painful. Differentiating goals from aspirations can really take the sting out of failure, making it less painful. More importantly, this differentiation can be used to use failure as a learning, for self-evaluation, and as a stepping stone to fulfil our aspirations.

7. PROCRASTINATION: DO FAILURES FORCE US TO DELAY IMPORTANT DECISIONS?

Have you ever wondered why open-ended To Do lists fail? Or why the resolutions we make with much determination don't take off? To Do lists are dynamic. Every item is necessary. This means there is no order of preference and anything that is *do-able* can be completed. Like a question paper in which all questions carry equal marks and there is no specified order in which to answer. Naturally the tendency is to attempt the do-able ones and skip the tougher ones with the intention of coming back to them later. The only trouble is that in real life the do-able ones dominate and we never do get back to the tougher ones. Of course, all questions do not carry equal marks either. Although the tasks are less important and often petty, do-able jobs hog our time. While we have the satisfaction of accomplishing most of the list, the important tasks remain undone. Often, these tasks end up as permanent items, being are carried forward whenever the next list is made.

The reason we are drawn to the petty jobs and derive pleasure in crossing them off the list is because we *need* them as a distraction from the really important ones. A simple solution is to make two lists: a Tough Jobs list and a Do-able list. It is not that we have forgotten these jobs or we are not aware of their importance, the fact is we have consciously chosen to ignore them, using the do-able list to hide behind. Procrastination is explained as deliberately searching for distractions to avoid doing unpleasant or difficult tasks. We know we have to decide. We know what we have to decide. And we also know that the after-effects are not going to be pleasant. So we delay the inevitable.

Why do we play the delay game? Perhaps an alternative that needs to be explored. Or maybe it is the rebel in us who refuses to abide by the rules. There could be a host of reasons behind our delaying behaviour but does failure or success have a role to play? Do our encounters with failure make us delay important decisions while successful ones boost faster decision-making? There is little doubt that failure slows us down. More importantly the fear of failure acts as a strong de-motivating force, sapping our self-confidence.

It was my fear of failure that first kept me from attempting the master work. Now, I'm beginning what I could have started ten years ago. But I'm happy at least that I didn't wait twenty years. ~ Paulo Coelho

The things we keep pushing for later are often linked to our fears: fear of failing, fear of change or the fear of the unknown. The interesting thing is that even when we cannot identify our fear, a flag is raised at the back of our minds, triggering a defense mechanism. The conscious mind reflects this when we push procrastinate over the tough Jobs list. The fear factor is heightened immediately after experiencing failure, putting the brakes on and holding up critical decisions.

8. THE FAILURE CHECKLIST

Have you achieved a successful failure or did you fail yourself and check-out?

SELF-BELIEF AND FEAR

- ✓ A deeper voice in my heart saying I would fail.
- ✓ I did not commit completely to the project.
- ✓ I aborted my plans halfway because of the fear of failing.
- ✓ I didn't seek enough help being egoistical/ fearing rejection.
- ✓ I didn't risk big because I felt it would lead to failure.

MORAL ISSUES

- ✓ I gave in to early gratifications and forgot discipline.
- ✓ I procrastinated and kept decisions on hold.
- ✓ I am sensitive and get hurt easily by criticism.
- ✓ If someone I seek help from says 'No', I never approach them again.

RISKS

- ✓ I have a reputation to protect. I cannot take risks and fail.
- ✓ I cannot afford to take risks and lose big. I am comfortable, why spoil it all?
- ✓ I began to believe that some factor was sure to trigger failure. This made me fearful and lowered my morale.

Success and Failure are not two different directions. They are stretches on the same road, differing only in frequency and duration. All you need to do is to drive through the rough patches.

9. FAILURE: THE DEFAULT OPTION

We can change the option of failure by choosing *to change; by endurance; by learning from it.*

Why are we shocked when failure strikes? Because we believe failure will never happen to us and we are assured of success.

Even when there is fear of failure in our hearts, we ignore it and go on.

Didn't we discuss fear being a deterrent and overcoming it? Absolutely. Fear of failure must be overcome, not brushed under the carpet. Everything we do has risk factors attached. But over the years we have learned from our failures how to eliminate those risks. The risks remain but we succeed not by overlooking or ignoring them, but by preparing.

We deal with the fear of failing by expecting and preparing for it. The war is always on. Consciously or unconsciously, we are always fighting fear. Precautions, planning and innovating are aspects of this eternal conflict. So when failure strikes, we are not shocked senseless. Stirred perhaps, but certainly not shaken.

The first thing we do while planning an activity is look for the failure risks. We identify possible fault lines and provide for them. Do we plan to fail? Certainly not. We plan to *prevent* failure. 'If you want to succeed, double your failure rate,' said Thomas J Watson, Founder of IBM. What he meant was that the more you fail the more you learn, and the more you learn the more prepared you become to handle failure. Failing-learning-success is a natural sequence when trying anything new. It is called the learning curve. As a rule, when working in a niche area, it is difficult to achieve success without first tripping. It would be like expecting a child to sprint when taking his first steps. Every process/job/profession has a learning curve. People will make mistakes before mastering it. Sometimes we can bypass or shorten that curve by anticipating and learning from others, but we cannot be fault-free.

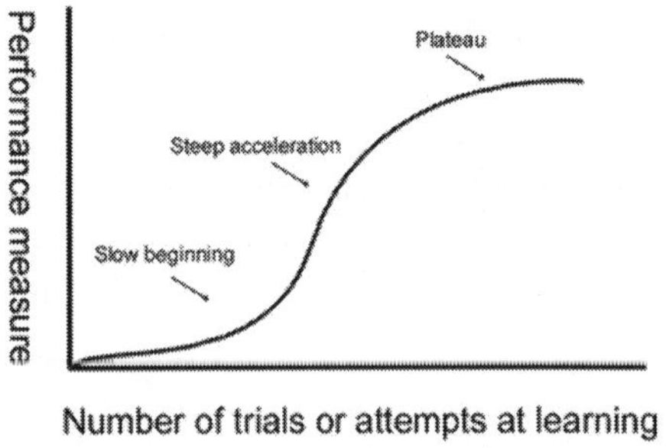

A typical learning curve shows a slow beginning with more failures. These decrease as we learn from our previous experiences.

Failure can be an important entry on your resume and shouldn't be looked at with scepticism. It tells the reviewer the applicant has faced failure and recovered; that he knows how to handle failure. Given a situation where risks are expected, he is a better bet than a person with a straight graph.

A young man asked Socrates the secret to success. In reply, Socrates asked the young man to meet him near the river the next morning. When they met, Socrates asked the young man to walk with him towards the river. When the water rose to their necks, Socrates ducked the young man under the water. The man struggled but Socrates was strong and kept him there until he started turning blue. Then Socrates pulled him out. The young man gasped and took a deep breath.

Socrates asked, 'What did you want most when you were down there?' The man replied, 'Air'. Socrates said, 'That is the secret to success. When you want success as badly as you want air, then you will get it.'

Many on our celebrity F list faced so much failure that they sought success just to survive. They needed success as desperately as they needed air to breathe. Determination can come from die hard passion, or from sheer desperation.

10. ATTITUDE: THE BEST RESOURCE

Success or failure is a factor of opportunity and resources. Indeed, there can be litte doubt that people with better access to resources have an advantage over those who do not. But even the best resources and opportunities fail to guarantee success. But what do resources include – money, social status, education. We seldom speak of attitude being a resource.

How valuable is attitide in creating game-changing conditions? Does the right attidue make the critical difference between success and failure?The right attitude can indeed be the biggest resource a person can have. History is full of stories of people overcame material, educational and social disadvantages to create opportunities for themselves on the strength of their attitude, just as many priviledged individuals have failed because they lacked the right attitude to life.

Society creates the environment in which attitudes develop. What then is attitude? It is our evaluation and reaction to people, events, ideas, objects, relationships and values, whether positive or negative. Attitude is what helps us find the silverlining and motivates us to learn from our failures. It is what drives us to create and achieve,or be content with what we have. Attiude is the difference between staying put, working hard or giving up.

Why do some societies progress while others continue to live in the past? There are many reasons but an important one is attitude. Some cultures are known to promote risk-taking. When a large number of people from a society or culture show a similarity in their attitude to life, we can assume it is part of their development. Attitudes can be learned, cultivated and changed. Risk-loving attitudes develop adventurous spirits and a love of exploring ideas and concepts, while risk-averse cultures opt for safety.

II. THE INDIAN 'F' LIST: FAMOUS FAILURES

A word about the list you are about to read. The list is not about people who had a launch pad and became become billionaires ('millionaire' seems to have lost its charm in these inflationary times). Neither is it about the rags to riches stories of people whose life has moved in more or less a single direction – up. So we are looking here, at people whose graphs have seen tremendous ups and downs – like an N or a W. This is therefore a turnaround list.

All these people had one common theme – hard work and dedication, but there were other parameters too. Some of the turnarounds happened because circumstances changed, creating appreciation for their work, others happened because they were 'discovered' by enlightened people (mentors). Some of our list simply got bored doing whatever they were doing and decided to put their energies into more interesting pursuits.

Guru Baba Nanak: This mystic-saint could not bring himself to lead the life of a merchant. His predicament is described in the famous story, *Sachha Sauda* (The True Deal), where a young Nanak he is sent to the market to buy goods. He meets a group of hermits and spends all his capital in serving them.

Rabindranath Tagore: The first non-European Nobel Laureate (Literature), was home schooled. At 17, he was sent to England for formal schooling, but didn't complete his studies.

Mahatma Gandhi: He failed to establish his practice as a lawyer in Bombay and then in Rajkot. In fact, he could not argue his first case and fled the courtroom with stage fright.

Milkha Singh: He survived at the Old Delhi railway station without food for three days. He was also imprisoned for travelling without a ticket between Shahdara and Delhi as he didn't have the ticket amount of two paisa. The fine was Rupees 2.5-3. They put him behind bars. His sister sold her earrings to bail him out. He was rejected by the Army thrice before he got in through the recommendation of his elder brother. Displaced during the partition of India, a dejected Milkha considered becoming a dacoit. A failure in early life, Singh went on to become a sporting legend and an inspiration for the young.

Amitabh Bachchan: The icon of Indian cinema, best known for his rich baritone voice, was rejected for an announcer's job with All India Radio because his voice was 'unsuitable'.

A.R. Rahman: A high school drop-out, he captured the imagination of India by becoming a leading composer-singer.

Gulzar: Starting off as a car mechanic, he became an acclaimed poet, director, lyricist and playwright.

Narendra Modi: He rose from being a tea-seller to becoming Prime Minister of India. As a child, Modi ran a tea stall with his brother, at Vadnagar railway station, Gujarat. His school teachers remember him as an average student.

Khushwant Singh: A failed lawyer, he tried his hand at All India Radio and the Indian Foreign Service before finally finding his calling as an author.

Sachin Tendulkar: This cricketing legend, Member of Parliament, and Bharat Ratna awardee, had to choose between education and a career in sports. He wished to be a fast bowler but the great Dennis Lille was left unimpressed and asked him to focus on in his batting.

Indira Gandhi: One of the most charismatic leaders independent India has seen, was dubbed *Gungi Gudia* (mute doll), in her early years as a politician. She became Prime Minister of India, quelling dissent in her own party, as well as the opposition. The mute doll went on to become one of India's toughest leaders, with the Western press calling her the Iron Lady.

12. RISKS

Are successful people more inclined to take risks? The fact is that nothing could be further from the truth. Successful people are likely to become the most risk-averse and typically go to all lengths to protect their success record. They do not wish to break their winning spree. And what is the *mantra* for that? Play safe and avoid risk at any cost. They may have been brave enough at some point in their lives, or just plain lucky, but once success *happened*, they lost all interest in being heroes and hastened out of the high risk zone.

And what of those who have a past history of failing? They have nothing to lose but their failure tag, no glory to protect, and everything to gain. Once they overcome their initial shock about failing (a tough nut to crack), such people are likely to take risks head on. This explains why the most spectacular successes have a back history of failure.

13. LOWER/MIDDLE/UPPER CLASS PERCEPTIONSOF FAILURE

While there are sub-divisions within these categories, we shall use three broad divisions – Upper, Middle and Lower Class.

Lower Class			Middle Class			Upper Class		
lower	middle	upper	lower	Upper	middle	lower	upper	middle

Survival Security Legacy

Traditionally, the lower classes worked, the upper class were the nobility, and the middle classes were the *bourgeoisie*. Professions such as law, medicine, engineering, accounting and teaching were dominated by the middle class. How do social classes perceive and handle failure? Why is it that the middle class rarely throws up dramatic success stories? Conversely, why do such stories come from the lower or upper classes? Is it an aversion to risk among the middle class? Do the poverty stricken take greater risks because they have less to lose or because they believe it to be a matter of survival? This social segment contributes the most rags-to-riches stories. These people are generally down-to-earth, hardworking, and often willing to interpret the law according to their plans, so justifying their actions. They rarely take the high moral ground if it keeps them from achieving success.

The upper class believes they have a legacy to protect. They move upwards, creating more and leaving more for the next generations. They are driven towards high-risk high-reward investments. They have enough capital to cover the risks which makes it affordable to lose. Like the lower class, they do not shy away from breaking or bending the rules to change the course of events in their favour, or allow norms to come between them and their objectives.

The middle class is perhaps the most risk averse risk and live in continuous fear of falling to lower class status. They try to maintain their middle status while differentiating themselves from the lower segment and pandering to the upper class. The middle class also dreads failure the most and looks for low-risk, assured returns in both economic and social scenarios. In choosing careers, they opt for the safe havens of advanced/professional education which translates into assured employment. In social set-ups, this class uses ethics and morality as a tool to maintain its integrity. Consequently the middle class is also the conscience of a society. It enforces social restrictions, thereby often limiting its own growth. Undoubtedly, the middle class is the soul of society. They also forms the manager/administrator segment in the corporate and bureaucratic world.

More importantly, this group is the least likely to contribute to innovations, fearing the risk of failure. 'What if I fail?' and 'I cannot afford to fail,' are thoughts that dominate the middle class. And the best way to secure a no-loss scenario is to avoid failure by playing safe and selecting activities that minimize risk. Parents choose activities that minimize exposure to accidents, shunning contact sports and two-wheelers, and even delaying car driving. Instead, they pamper their children with safe activities, frequenting movies, dining out and cultural events – the very things teenagers love to loathe.

The middle class sees failure as a threat to their survival. So how does it react when failure *does* strike? Of all the socio-economic classes, the middle class finds it hardest to handle and experience the most pain. Due to their deep fear of failure, bordering on paranoia, parents do not provide sufficient *learn by failing* opportunities to their children. So when failure comes, it hits them hard. Since they lack previous exposure to failure, they do not know how to react. Many panic or turn violent, hurting themselves or those around them.

14. SUCCESS: JUST A NUMBERS GAME

Measurement is the first step that leads to control and eventually to improvement. If you can't measure something, you can't understand it. If you can't understand it, you can't control it. If you can't control it, you can't improve it. ~ H. James Harrington

Why is failure or success all about numbers? Why can't life be about being happy, rather than not being happy? Why can't we let happiness be the measure of our lives? Yet, numbers rule our lives. All human endeavour, aspirations and potential have been reduced to numbers. They decide whether we are successes or failures; if we are fit for a job or not; whether we can experience the joys of being alive or be miserable.

A child is assigned a number as soon as he is born. In school he cannot achieve knowledge without numbers. As an adult, his life is governed by numbers. In the office, in shops, on the soccer field, in a queue, we just cannot escape numbers. Governments get elected and fall on numbers. Even the heart beats a certain number of times and the lungs have their own number of inflations and deflations.

Harrington says that if you can't measure something, you can't understand it. But can love and compassion be converted into numbers? Or faith? Yet we *do* understand these concepts. So how can happiness be converted into numbers?

Instead of focusing on *why* and *what*, we have trained our minds to look for *how much* and *how many*. Anyone who has satisfactory answers to these two queries can go places. Whether he can answer the *why's* and *what's* don't seem to matter, as their significance is always lower than *how much* and *how many*.

15. GAMES WE PLAY

Remember those innocent looking game stalls in carnivals and fetes; how seemingly easy tasks promised attractive returns, drawing children in hoards; how most of them narrowly missed achieving the target but came running back with more coupons to try again? The kids did not know the odds stacked against them. They continued to try till they ran out of funds. There are few winners but many parents buying cheer-up gifts for disappointed kids. *These games are designed for failure.* So how do some win? There is a particular way to break the pyramid of tumblers or make the coin fall into the right slot, which children learn by chance. Once the organizers realize their secret is out, they stop the game. Their philosophy is simple: We are here to make money. If everyone wins, we lose. A lesson in free markets.

The biggest carnival that sees grown-ups flocking to it in millions, is the stock market. The task is simple – you buy a script, it rises and you sell to make a profit. If it falls, you arrange for more money. This seemingly simple task has caused people to lose their entire life's savings, as well those of people who trusted them with their money. It is only when they have lost everything and reminisce how close they were to the jackpot that they realize that the task was not that simple after all. Some gain enlightenment when it dawns on them that this game is designed for people to lose. The undisclosed truth is the game collects money by making people believe there is a grand prize to be won. The only people who really gain are those who control the game – the stock operators, the brokers, and of course, the government which taxes the transactions. For the rest, it is difficult to gain. Not that there is never a win. But winning only draws them deeper into the game, till they have invested everything. There is only one way the person on the street can make money from stocks – by understanding the business, by tracking company developments and evaluating threats and growth prospects. Owning stock is like becoming a partner in that company. You thrive by nurturing it.

Simple things often prove difficult to handle and result in failure. One seemingly simple thing which most people get wrong is relationships. Relationships are perhaps the most important ventures anyone can involve himself in, and undoubtedly the most difficult to maintain.

Predictably, relationships see the most failures. We spend resources in terms of emotion, time and money on nurturing a relationship. We often change our lifestyles and behavior to accommodate the other person. Sometimes we become so attached that we are ready to adapt to a different culture and even religion, letting go of our own. In spite of this, many people struggle to keep going, stumble, and fail. Years of precious inputs can become naught through a single act of emotional turbulence. Relationships can be the most rewarding investments a person makes, but they can also be the most risky, beating the volatilities of the stock market.

16. WHY RELATIONSHIPS FAIL (OR SUCCEED)

This is perhaps the most talked about topic, with everyone having his own reason to explain failure. And each reason may be right for people speak from their own experience. But can we identify one factor that contributes in making or breaking a relationship?

FAMILY VS CORPORATE ATTITUDE

A corporation is an efficient workplace. There is an established chain of command. Roles and duties are defined. Everyone is expected to perform efficiently. What is the central force that binds a corporation? What makes everyone report to duty every morning and perform his allocated duties? Work ethic? Work culture? Honesty? Integrity? Diligence? Management pressure? Rules? Perhaps all of these, but these are not *the* reason for reporting to work when it is your three-year olds birthday or a beautiful sun is spreading its warmth on a winter morning. No, the real reason is: Need. We need something and the company can provide the resources for it; in return we perform the roles and duties allocated to us. Corporations work on the principle of need. They need you and you need the job. If you do not do your job efficiently or honestly, they will replace you.

But that's not how families run. Even though we take pride in running offices like a family, the fact is they have different requirements which have to be fulfilled differently. We do not talk of efficient families do we? We speak of loving and caring homes. Why do mothers get up at 4 am on freezing winter mornings to prepare lunch boxes for their children and then see them off to school? Is it *need*? The right answer is because they *want* to.

When families are run like corporate offices, the chances are there are relationship issues. Families are bound with emotion. They run on values. The moment emotions give way to need-based bonding, trouble starts. I-give-therefore-I-demand does not work where love and compassion are the de facto standard. An even more disastrous situation is expecting a return on emotional expectations (ROEE). Most relationships enter troubled waters when we begin expecting something in return. Placing a barter tag on our love weakens the relationship.

A mother wants her child to have the right food and environment for healthy growth. But more than anything, she wants her child to be happy. Her wishes and actions remain the same despite the passing years. A family that gives to one another without expecting anything in return, has strong bonds.

We need to understand the difference between accountability and responsibility. Accountability works on a master-slave equation, a work-for-returns basis. Accountability works by creating an environment of fear – fear of not living up to a perception or self-image; fear of performing poorly or getting caught. Working with responsibility, however, involves motivation to deliver. Rather than fear, it is driven by self-inspired zeal. Accountability involves adhering to the rules while responsibility involves going past the rulebook. An employee is accountable; a mother is responsible.

While it does becomes testing sometimes, if you move forward in a relationship with understanding and no demands, the relationship will become be strong enough to weather any storm.

AVATARS OF EXPECTATION

Expectations are not limited to what we want others to do. The scope widens to include what we want others to *be*. Parents plan for their children's future; they are entitled to do so. The trouble starts when they begin to impose their ideas on their kids. Often, parents try to make up for their personal failures and unfinished dreams through their children. They believe that pursuing a particular path will give happiness to their young ones. The children may, of course, have their own paths to happiness. Khaled Hosseini captures the essence of the situation in his book, *The Kite Runner*, when one of its characters says, 'Children are not colouring books. You don't get to fill them with your favourite colours.'

People often develop an ideal picture of their partner. Couples wish their other half to conform to this image. But when they do not and appear as a bundle of imperfections, then one or both are disappointed. What happens then? They may compromise and modify their ideal picture. But if they fail to adjust their expectations, the relationship will come under fire. The disappointed partner may even look for the ideal image outside their relationship. Issues such as infidelity are actually rooted in the expectations we have of others. What happens when expectations go unfulfilled? It has the potential to break hearts and crash the stock market.

NOT A MATTER OF CONTROL

We treat the people around us as extensions of ourselves. It is a matter of trust. When we ask them to do something, we expect that they will do it as we would. When they do not, it irritates us. Not because the other person has performed badly but because our faith in our extension has failed. It is not about exercising control over another person but the failure of our trust that rattles us – manifesting as irritation, disillusionment and anger. Delegation is simply an extension of the self as we empower others to act on our behalf. Any error or failure by the delegate is seen as our failure. It has to be replaced with us, we and ours. It is an evolutionary step to a lasting and meaningful personality.

SHOE SIZE

It is a popular belief in India that when the shoe size of a son matches his father's, it is time for the father to realise his son has grown up and that needs to treat his son as a friend, an equal. It is a signal that the time has come when he can no longer command or scold him. Like a friend, the father can only make a request or convince him with reason.

Unfortunately, most fathers forget these words of wisdom. They continue as they did, not realising their sons have grown up. Most father-son relationships come under strain during this stage. Fathers complain their sons do not listen to them and disobey them on purpose. What fathers have to realize is that their sons wish to be treated as adults and will not accept advice if treated as a child. Sons thus reject authority and rebel. It is time for fathers to change from parent to friend. All you have to do is keep track of the shoe sizes.

17. PEER POWER

How often have you struggled to choose between your favourite activity (reading, listening to music, painting, sport) and what your friends are doing? How often have you chosen to do something you do not enjoy, just to fit in? Why do people give in to peer pressure? Does it play a role in determining our success or failure as child, adolescent and adult?

Four distinct pressure groups influence a child –parents, pressure siblings, teachers and peers. While parental, sibling and teacher pressures decline with age, peer pressure continues to mark its presence in the various stages of our lives, being most dominant n our adolescent years. Usually perceived as a negative influence, peer pressure has different aspects. Peer pressure is about handling criticism and conforming to the norms of the social group to which you belong. Often, the urge to conform leads to giving up your personal choices and values, or doubting your own views. Ultimately, we go with the majority, thereby adapting to the character norms and values of the group.

How strong is the pressure to conform? In 1951, Solomon Asch conducted a series of experiments which demonstrated the degree to which an individual's opinions are influenced by the majority group.

Asch conformity experiments or the Asch Paradigm, as they came to be known in social psychology, claimed that most participants got to the point where they realized they must be wrong and the majority right. The participants also exhibited a 'distortion of action', suggesting they knew what the correct answer was but conformed with the majority simply because they didn't want to seem inferior. Can we put a number to it? The experiments found that at some point, 75% of the participants went with the group, which was wrong.

How does peer pressure actually affect our lives? Sometimes in seemingly harmless ways such as going to the movies when you wanted quiet time at home or having a particular haircut. But peer pressure can be serious and influence our college and career choices (all my friends are going there), as well as extremely dangerous, addictive and life-threatening habits such as smoking, alcoholism, drugs and antisocial activities. This is the pressure that most young adults find difficult to resist because in some part of their minds they don't *want* to resist. The only reason I signed up for Facebook and WhatsApp was because of the rest of the gang – pure peer pressure. I could have resisted but I found myself joining the group. Then I became an online addict. Substitute Facebook with any other substance/item/concept/ideology/cult, and you will get an idea of the power your peers have over you.

Of course, peer power can work both ways. The greatest social changes – revolutions, re-organizations, new ideas (including Facebook), have succeeded because of passion and peer pressure. It can turn around your life, change your rhythm and infuse new life. 'The people you hang around with can make or break your life. Choose them carefully,' my father used to say. But do we really have a choice? Or the wisdom? Peer pressure can express itself non-verbally, without coming into direct contact. It can incite the desire for conformity from a distance, affecting us like a weapon of mass destruction (WMD). Perhaps that is why we have parents. The craving for social acceptance is far greater during adolescence. It is the time when we are looking for adventure and want to do something different. We rebel against traditional ways and impose conformity among our peers. In that delicate age of change, we take critical and life-changing decisions. Some of those we cherish. Others we live to regret. Peer pressure was key in both cases.

Do immigrants have a better chance of succeeding? What happens when we are removed from our homeland? Does it free us from the boundaries set tradition? Yes. Migrating to a new land, whether intra-country, small town to big city, or inter-country, it gives us the opportunity to free ourselves from the legacy and traditions of the society in which we were born. Many reasons, apart from better opportunities, fuel the decision to migrate, such as political tensions (the holocaust forced millions of Jews to leave their lands in order to survive; the Punjabis were driven from their homes following the partition of India.

One reason why immigrants succeed is because they leave behind false pride and are willing to do any job. Often, we turn away from opportunities which we feel to be beneath us, because of social pressure. But in a new land migrants leave their inhibitions behind and pursue any opportunity which presents itself. Things that were undoable or unthinkable because of social pressures, are seen as opportunities. Migrants are freed from peer pressure until such time they develop new peers. Anonymity has its own advantages as often, it is community pressure that keeps us from succeeding.

18. LADY LUCK OR PROBABILITY: THE K-FACTOR SUCCESS THEORY

If you believe in luck, the chances are that you also believe in religion. You have to believe in religion simply because there are so many things that can go wrong, so many links that can fail. Such is the complexity of life that we often wonder why a certain person, company or system succeeds, when others doing the same thing in the same way, do not. Why do some people succeed while others fail? We hear of cases when it all came together for someone to lead a creative life. Then we think of those who just could not get it right. Was it a broken link in the chain?

Searching for a success formula leads us to explore different aspects of humanity. One journey takes us into the realm of the cosmos and spirituality. It is said that if we wish for something from the depths of our hearts and pursue it with all our passion, then cosmos conspires to make it happen. The elements of the cosmos will create opportunities repeatedly for us to succeed. This belief, though it defies scientific logic, is a positive one as it creates no mental blocks to success. Scientists find it difficult to accept this view but then, many unexplained things do happen. Science has a word: Probability. But humans continue to search for a formula for success and believe, even if it defies logic.

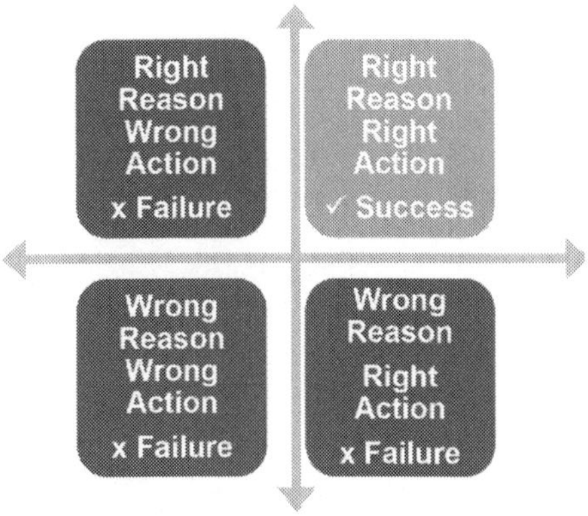

One theory says that we achieve success when right actions are matched withright thoughts. We do things every day for different reasons, including compulsion, anger, hope or frustration, and often failure. Sometimes we do the right thing for dubious motives or our intentions are good but they not followed by right action. Right intentions need to be backed by right actions.

19. IQ: MISMEASURE OF THE MAN

For over a hundred years since it was first devised, Intelligence Quotient (IQ), has come to mean how intelligent someone is. The higher the numeric score, the more intelligent a person is understood to be. How is it done? The IQ of an individual is a relative measure within a representative group. A test is done with group of children or adults as a representative sample. An average score is arrived at. An individual's score is then compared against this average score.

MENTAL AGE, CHRONOLOGICAL AGE AND IQ

Mental Age /Chronological Age X 100 = Intelligence Quotient

A 6-year-young child (chronological age) who can do activities recorded for the same age group (mental age), will have an IQ of 100. The score comes with an adjustment factor called standard deviation of 15.The majority of people have an IQ which is either 15 above or below this number, i.e. between 85 and 115. Scores below 85would indicate weak mental abilities while above 115 would mean superior intelligence. Some of the takeaways are:

- IQ is a relative measure of intelligence. In other words, the intelligence of a person is measured in relation to the average intelligence of a group.
- IQ is different for different age groups, cultural groups and even gender groups.
- IQ differs from region to region and country to country, depending on the representative sample. Each country has its own IQ average.

Despite these variations (and in the absence of a better alternative), IQ has established itself as the standard measurement for intelligence. In the 1990s, James Flynn presented some interesting observations. He noticed that when the current generation took an IQ test designed for an earlier generation, the current generation performed significantly better than their elders. The difference was so dramatic that if the two results (of the older and the current generation) were compared, the current generation stood out as geniuses. The grandparent generation fell back as 'mentally challenged'. This meant that over generations, we have gained a tremendous degree of intelligence.

Flynn established that this increase was a linear in nature (every successive generation appeared smarter than the previous one). This observation prompted him to ask why our IQ levels are higher than that if our grandparents? His observations came to be known as the Flynn Effect and has confounded psychologists ever since. Among the possible explanations psychologists came up with was, better and more hours of schooling. While the jury is still out on this, we can safely add other takeaways

- IQ is not a static number; intelligence for a region or country can improve over time.
- Activities like increased education and engaging the mind in special activities (computer games for instance), leads to an increase in IQ.
- The association of IQ with genetics is questionable since the same genetic pool shows vast difference in IQ level over generations.

In July 2012, it was reported that ever since the IQ system began, the IQ level of women were less than men. That is, till now. For the first time, women have scored *more* on IQ level tests than men. Flynn, who published the results, attributed this change to the 'complexity of the modern world', with women taking up career roles in addition to being home-makers. Although the complexities have risen for both sexes, it has worked as an equalizer, favouring women, who were clearly at a disadvantage earlier. Technological advancement and the opening up of cultures have enabled women to devote more hours to study, particularly the subjects used to measure IQ. Hence, placing women below men on the intelligence scale was primarily because of the nature of their engagements (focusing on different aspects of life). The results have clearly indicated the shift by women to IQ testing-friendly subjects.

- The takeaway is that the measurement of IQ is subjective in nature. It is not a true measure of human intelligence. At best IQ is a partial measure. It is certainly not an adequate tool to segregate the gifted from the morons. The different dimensions of intelligence, is ignored by IQ testing.

This brings us to the central issues: *what intelligence* does IQ testing measure? To answer this we need to understand what intelligence is. While it would be foolish to attempt to define the complex nature of intelligence, it can be said that human intelligence goes far beyond IQ evaluations which have already created schisms in society by placing people in narrow bands. While the best human minds are still debating what intelligence is, IQ has caused biases against people who were inadequately or wrongly measured. Clearly, the IQ system is guilty of mismeasuring the human mind and needs to be overhauled or debunked at the earliest. Apart from analytical, logic, reasoning and language skills, we need to explore and distinguish between *intelligence, knowledge, memorization and wisdom*, all of which are essential elements of intellect. It is only when we consider all these elements that we can achieve some clarity about what intelligence is and how to measure it (if we need to measure it at all).

IQ testing has done more harm than good. A part of the population has been humiliated, separated from their friends, sidelined and even put in special care, simply because they were evaluated to have lower intelligence. It is difficult to believe that IQ evaluation was originally devised by Alfred Binet, to identify and help children with possible learning disabilities. What it has done is to weed out children with lower IQ levels while increasing the focus on those with higher scores. Instead of getting more attention, children with lower scores suffer from the stigma of being branded as dumb. Besides this, through segregation, they also lose out on the opportunity of learning in the company of their brighter peers. The brighter ones are not a happy lot either. They suffer from the burden of expectations – to perform well and increase their scores. The pressure to deliver is not easy to take and often results in stress, sometimes to breaking point.

Despite human advancement, we still do not have a defined policy to handle children. We flip-flop between modernity and tradition. After subjecting them to a century of relentless evaluations, we have still failed our children.

20. MATURITY VS TALENT

Consider a class of 40 students. The difference between the youngest and the eldest child is as high as eleven months. The older children are usually better at picking up the topics discussed and they set the pace of teaching. The younger, less mature children are seen as slowing down the pace of learning. Teachers work under time constraints, struggling to keep up with the schedule. They simply do not have the time to satisfy the needs of every student. So every new topic is followed by a quick review session, which is dominated by the cream of the class. This cream comprises those with a greater grasping power and quicker understanding of concepts. They are thus considered 'intelligent'. This 'intelligent' group speaks for the whole class, leaving the slower ones to fend for themselves. And it is not by chance that this intelligent group has children with a higher maturity level. The younger lot remain at a disadvantage. The performance evaluators, however, do not consider the maturity factor while grading students. As a result, the younger lot usually appear to be underperformers, underachievers, or even failures.

This process begins in Class1, when the child is five years old and lasts till he is 17 and leaves school. Session after session a child is branded a failure or under-performer, simply because of a system that measures his development and performance against a group of more mature children. It is nothing short of delivering blow after blow to the psyche of that child. The blows only become more powerful with time, carrying more humiliation and mental agony. Some are so severely affected that they drop out of school or even taking the extreme step of ending their lives.

The fact is that the only difference between the so called slow learners and achievers is that they happen to be inappropriately grouped. The first group would develop into the second, given adequate time and space to grow. In an ideal scenario, a class should comprise of children with minimal age difference. Each class would need perhaps 12 sections. Since this would put considerable logistical pressure on the school's resources, it would be unviable. We can, however, narrow the difference between the eldest and youngest child in a class to six months, thus eliminating any unfair advantage because of age. There are no dumb students; there are only different levels of maturity.

21. THE BURDEN OF LEGACY: WHY CELEBRITY CHILDREN FAIL

We have a tendency to think in continuity. If something good is happening, we believe it to be a trend which will continue, and the future will be even better. On the other hand, if someone is passing through hard times, we expect even darker times ahead. The general perception is that happy leads to happier and hard leads to harder. If we draw a graph between time and happiness (or sadness), we have a tendency to extend the line, extrapolate or interpolate. The prospects of future wellbeing and security creates a euphoric lifting of our spirits, while thinking of dark days ahead pushes us down into depression.

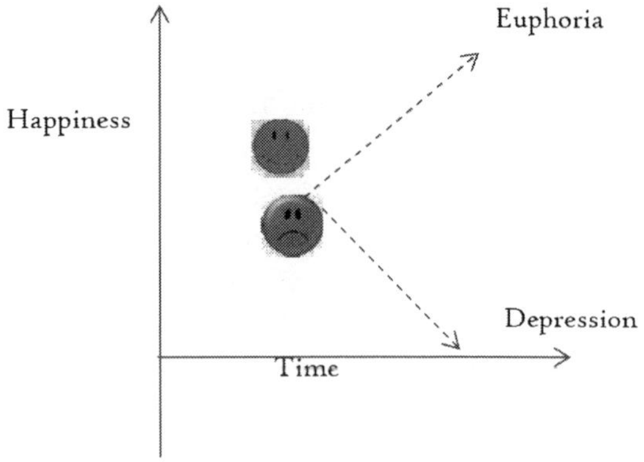

We love to predict the outcome of events; such line extensions are common to us, be it in relationships, emotions or the stock market.

With celebrity families, we think how lucky the children are. We are certain they will naturally become celebrities themselves. Children of politicians will become excellent statesmen, children of movie stars will win hearts on the screen, children of sports persons will get us medals in the Olympics and set new records of human endurance, children of famous business personalities who revolutionized the industry will continue the innovative approach and the children of doctors will serve humanity. We are, of course, extra cautious in dealing with the children of murderers, alcoholics, drug addicts and those who failed in their lives, as the children too, are considered threats to society. The general perception is that given the best resources available to them, the children of celebrities will certainly do well.

However, we know for sure that all good things come to an end and that the worst of times does not last. This holds for people as well people. This means that our predictions of eternal happiness or doom are both wrong. How wrong we are when we predict a future for people based on their lineage. Why do children of celebrities seem to fail? The truth is it is the parents who fail and the children are the results of that failure. The kids suffer as they either explode or implode.

EXPLOSION

One reason, undoubtedly an important one, why we believe someone does well in life, is access to material resources). In the race for fame, celebrity parents have to choose between parenting and generating resources. Unfortunately, many choose to maintain their celebrity status, generate resources, and end up outsourcing the parenting process. Since they cannot be there personally, they try to replace parenting by providing material happiness. So the poor little rich boys (and girls), get toys to play with and an army of caregivers to boss over. This resource-funded parenting, however, fails to work, as all the resources in the world cannot replace the personal attention parents can give their children.

IMPLOSION

Perhaps the most cogent reason why we are shocked to see celebrity kids fail, is because we have viewed them as winners from the day they were born. They are born into the spotlight, amid high hopes and expectations as 'the heirs'. We expect the stardom of the parents to be transferred to their children. Comparison with their celebrity parent/s results in great expectations from star kids. We forget the struggles and failures their parents underwent as the heavy cost of stardom. We assume the parents will transfer their knowledge and skills to their children. Such a transfer is possible with computers but not with humans. Every child has to go through the same learning or formatting process, experiencing success and failure on their own.

Star kids, however, are not allowed to quit or fail. Such is the pressure of expectations, to succeed, that all possible resources are mobilized to prevent failure. The star kids themselves become aware of these expectations to deliver and many become overwhelmed, and implode.

PART V: THE PSYCHOLOGY OF FAILURE

Life is a series of successes and failures. We need to survive and thrive in both cases. But we rarely learn as much from our successes as we do from our failures. We do not stop to think *why* we succeeded – perhaps because we are too busy celebrating. Did we really do everything right or did it just fall into place by chance? Was our success expected, the result of a well thought out plan or did we win because our opponents double-faulted? Can our success be repeated? Interestingly, when it comes to choosing our role models, we are naturally inclined to choose successful people we wish to emulate, without understanding *what* made them succeed. Success is a poor teacher. Failure, however, is a hard task master. It drills lessons into us and doesn't let us forget. Every time we are about to commit the same mistake, previous failure reminds us of the pain.

We have museums and study courses on leaders like Mahatma Gandhi, so that generations can learn from his life. But few Gandhis emerge. I have never seen a course called 'What Made Gandhi Tick?' or Why Gandhi Succeeded'. More importantly, can we replicate his model for success? We continuously focus on his *lifestyle* and not on the factors that made him a success. Lifestyle is a matter of culture and convenience; people adopt different lifestyles according to their comfort levels.

Mohandas Gandhi is described as someone who was not a great scholar, nor was he a great warrior. He was not born with exceptional faculties. Neither was he a good orator or a great writer. He did not claim divine knowledge. He considered himself an average man with average abilities. Born into a middle class *bania* family in an obscure princely State of India, he was a mediocre student, shy and nervous. He could not muster the courage to speak in public. His first attempt at legal practice failed miserably. And yet he had his share of success.

Don't read success stories, you will only get a message. Read failure stories, you will get some ideas to get success, advised Dr APJ Abdul Kalam, former President of India. He knew; he had his share of failures. 'Over the years I had nurtured the hope to be able to fly to handle a machine as it rose higher and higher in the stratosphere was my dearest dream,' he wrote in his books, *Wings of Fire* and *My Journey: Transforming Dreams into Actions.* He applied to the Indian Air Force but was not selected. 'I had failed to realize my dream of becoming an air force pilot...I walked around for a while till I reached the edge of a cliff... before deciding to seek a new way forward... It is only when we are faced with failure do we realise that these resources were always there within us. We only need to find them and move on with our lives.' Kalam went on to put his 'heart and soul' into his job as Senior Scientific Assistant, and later came to be known as the Missile Man.

1. MONEY SUCCESS AND FAILURE

Money= Food
Money = Knowledge
Money = Independence
Not having Money = Not having Food, Independence and Knowledge = Failure

Money is arguably the best invention of man. But money is not eco-friendly. In earlier times, 'money' meant different things. It meant how many cows you held and it made you care for animals;

how much cultivable land you had, and that made you care for the land. 'Money' also meant developing relationships and caring for people, so that they would support you in times of need.

Then man invented modern money. All you needed to do was hoard it. There was no need to care for the land, the animals or people. Now anyone holding money could become rich. Wealth became transferable. In fact, it would not be wrong to say the transferability of money was the greatest invention of man. It changed the way we conduct our lives. Earlier, even if a man took over land by force, he still had to work it to make it produce; if a person stole a cow, he would have to tend to it. But transferable money was different. It meant anyone could snatch or steal the equivalent of an acre of produce or a month's milk supply from a cow, without doing any labour.

Gradually, even the requirement of developing relationships was eliminated because there were people who would work for money. To accumulate money became the only one goal for people. Money became associated with success. You were a success if you had accumulated a pile of money. Rich men began to employ people to look after their farms and animals, creating a layer of people between himself and the farm. Soon he employed more people to look after the accounts and to protect the land. Everything from goods to services was available, for money. With every new layer, the gap between the farm and the moneyed man increased, disconnecting him from the values of nature. The monetization of products, services and knowledge had everyone competing for a single resource - money -the master key that unlocked everything.

The result of this 'reduction process' was that every craft and emotion got reduced to a monetary value. Money becomes the measure of success. Someone with money could claim a status equivalent, or perhaps greater than, a person with knowledge, skill or character (or all three) but who did not hold the master key. Society acknowledged and followed this norm.

Once the norm was set, everybody followed. Accumulation of money became the sole objective and measure in society as the role of money changed from being a facilitator of services to the determining factor. This signalled the rot setting into society.

Money is not bad. The transferability of money is not bad. Even the monetization of goods and services is not bad. The rot sets in because *everything* is monetized. It becomes the root of all evil. Some things simply cannot be converted into money or monetized – such as love, trust and faith. Some things need to be valued in a different currency. It is when the same money is used to value *everything* that the trouble starts.

2. THE ROLE OF SOCIETY

It is the duty of society to decide what values to promote. Do we wish to monetize everything, thereby bringing all services and roles at par, or do we wish to separate noble activities and professions? A society which accords respect and status to teachers, scientists and doctors, progresses well while the society that puts these professions on par with stockbrokers and real estate agents, suffers. Unfortunately, the latter has become the reality.

Honouring the right type of people creates the right models for generations. Elevating those with the most money, as people to emulate, triggers a race to acquire money by any means. Since people would be interested in getting rich quickly, this would lead to low literacy and increased crime rates. Promoting knowledge-based professions, on the other hand, prompts the young to take up such carrier paths. Since all such professions are associated with a stiff learning curve, students would be exposed to failure as well as creating a more mature and nurtured generation, who understands the risks and values of life.

Treating failure as a stepping stone creates a more understanding and compassionate generation. Treating success as supreme and failure as not an option, we only push for a cruel generation engaged in a cut-throat competitive war with their own friends and brothers.

Fear of failure would rule. Such a society would be doomed. Knowledge-based professions would be sucked into a vicious vortex and engage in accumulating money. Teachers would train students to earn, instead of learn more. Doctors would treat their rich and poor patients according to their resources and not the disease. Nobody would trust anyone. Trust-deficit is a characteristic of an anarchic society ruled by the motto: 'Each one for himself'. Sadly, all these traits are discernable in society today. The result is only too predictable. As a people we must ask ourselves whether we want an anarchic or a compassionate society built on trust and humaneness? The option to fail or not rests with us. We must choose wisely.

SPORTPERSONS

Sport offers unique exposure to failure. Sports rules, by design, are formed to have a winner and a loser. And unless you are a bad loser, you have a lot to gain from the experience. Good sportspersons are generally seen as good losers. They accept defeat gracefully. They go through the whole process of pain and disappointment associated with a failure, but they come out pretty well. How do they do it?

Sportspersons understand success and failure. They are exposed to dose of success and failure, quickly. The more they play and *lose*, the sooner they complete their learning curve. Good sportspersons understand this. They play more games and learn from every game. Sportspersons are always testing their limits. Remember the Olympic motto: *Citius, Altius, Fortius* (Faster, Higher, Stronger)? It is meant to represent the human spirit, always testing the limits. Actually, sportsmen are testing failure limits. Every time they create a new record, they set a new failure limit at which human potential fails.

At the initial stages of the learning curve, losing a game is more important than winning. This is because winning will not provide the same opportunity to analyse mistakes. But if we win, why bother to analyse it? But how can we be sure that our victory was because of our superior play? Could it be that we won because the other team made more mistakes? Playing against a stronger team may not give a similar result. Perhaps the other team lost because they made a couple of self-goals. Another team may not oblige.

Winning gives us a sense of superiority that may be real or false, but in either case, prevents us from making up for our shortcomings and improving. Losing games provides us with opportunities to identify mistakes. Failure makes us humble. It deflates the balloon within winners and gets us back on the ground. Humility is good. Another interesting thing failure does, is it kills the fear of failing. Failing makes us immune to jitters. It allows us to improvise and take risks. The more we fail the less we are burdened by expectations.

On the other hand, if we have been winning all our lives, a single failure has the power to destroy us. We have never been through the hurricane before. As winners we never experienced pain. Over the years, winners build a perfectionist image. What a failure does is shatter that image. The devastation of pride hurts badly. Losing is painful. No one wants to fail but everyone wants to learn. Everyone *has* to learn. Not learning is not an option. We can learn in a classroom or on the field; lose a few games and *then* come back to the white board to learn more. Use failure as feedback.

Everyone should take up a sport either for character-building or as therapy. And I mean actually getting down to the field and playing, not sitting in front of the TV with snacks and a drink. If we want to really benefit from sport, we must get out our sport equipment and get going. Develop the mind-set of a sportsperson and the chances are we will be able to use failure to our advantage.

SCIENTISTS

Science does not fail but scientists do. And they may fail for a very long time. Scientists have a lifelong relationship with failure. All of science is based on observation and experimentation. Scientists present a hypothesis and do experiments to prove it. If the experiments fail, they reject or modify their hypothesis. A scientist can spend a lifetime in research without tasting success. He patently weathers failure after failure and continues. When Einstein said, 'Genius is 1% inspiration and 99% perspiration,' he captured the gist of scientific work. We imagine Nobel Laureats to be geniuses at work. But behind the glamour of the award lies the struggle and frustration s/he faced along the way. If anyone wants to know about failure and how to survive it, he need only read the life stories of scientists. But with every failure they evolve and improve.

More importantly, how do they survive failures for such a long time when they believe themselves to be on the right track? Their fundamental strength and perseverance lies in their basic training as scientists. They learn from failure they are not afraid of failure. They consider failure to be evolutionary steps, that's all. They live with the belief that if they stick with what they are doing, they will eventually try out all the options and succeed. Like Edison and his 10,000 attempts. Stick with it. Tweak a little and repeat. The more we sweat and fail, the more options for failure are eliminated. One day, they will get that 1% brainwave and wonders will happen. With every single failure, Edison inched closer to his final objective – electricity.

'One never notices what has been done; one can only see what remains to be done,' commented Marie Curie. All the scientists in the world seem to be on the same mental frequency. Curie's comment could easily for Edison. Scientists and sportsperson share a common understanding of failure and how to persevere. Both understand that the only way break the failure ceiling is by sticking to the routine. Keeping up with the drill will get them their 1%.

'Nothing in life is to be feared, it is only to be understood. Now is the time to understand more, so that we may fear less,' wrote Marie Curie, who devoted her life to science and was awarded two Nobel Prizes, in two different subjects. When she presented her initial work, no one was ready to accept that a *woman* was capable of such thought. Earlier, she was even denied admission to University in Poland because she was a female. When Marie and her husband, Pierre, won the Nobel Prize in Physics for their research into radiation, the prize money allowed Marie to take on her first lab assistant. Till then, she and Pierre had done all the toil personally. They worked for 10 years in a dilapidated converted shed next to the School of Physics and Chemistry. The shed, formerly a medical school dissecting room, was poorly ventilated and not even waterproof. They were unaware of the deleterious effects of radiation exposure attendant on their continued unprotected work with radioactive substances. Marie later died in a sanatorium, from the effects of radiation exposure in her unprotected lab and the mobile x-ray vans she operated for the Red Cross.

MUSICIANS

Another talent group that is highly exposed to failure are musicians. Apparently, the 99-1 ratio also applies to musicians. There is another thing musicians and scientists share – they both begin with belief but at some point in their 99% perspiration routine, they become so involved with their craft that when success comes it takes on a very different meaning from what they first imagined. Like any other interest group, scientists and musicians too, begin with the dream of making it big. Somewhere down the line, having failed for (say) 9900 times, their mental state changes, so when that 1% does happen, the experience is more on a spiritual level. What did Curie do with the prize money she got? Did she splurge? She hired an assistant and upgraded her lab. The prize money for her was a resource to do more research. Success has a deeper meaning when we get it after years of failure.

Science, sports and music can all help us weather failure better, especially the emotional and psychological setbacks. All these people start off with a dream to do achieve something. They become more interested in reaching that goal than in the applause and recognition which perhaps drove them earlier. Reaching the goal becomes their applause and motivator to do more.

How does this differ from a stock broker who, through practice, is better placed to handle financial failure? Money to a stock broker is seed to make more money. His dream does not transform mid- way. Every day his mountain of gold grows and his investors gain pleasure from watching it grow. Unless that resource is spread around and given to creators, it has no meaning. Unless we use resources to enable the Curies of the world to hire an assistant and upgrade their lab, that mountain of gold is simply locked treasure.

3. CULTURE, FAILURE AND RISK

Why do some individuals take more risks than others? Is it that what is true for an individual also holds true for communities, societies and nations? A nation is, after all, a group of cultures coexisting harmoniously. So why do some nations take more risks and are thus more progressive than others? How does culture affect our risk-taking abilities and attitude towards failure?

Cultures, where a strong sense of individualism prevails, are more likely to take risks, while those with strong collective value systems, tend to be more conservative and have lower risk-taking potential. Can we prove it? In the Eastern world, traditionally, families and communities provide strong support to individuals. In the individualistic societies of the Western world, this bond weakens as the individual tries to break free from society to establish his own identity. He is ready to break social norms, go against conventions, and try out new ideas. This urge to break free encourages taking risks and challenges. Consequently, the chances of failure also increase. But the more they fail, the more they learn to cope with it, and end with an overall higher success rate, seen in both the new inventions made, as well as in general prosperity.

In traditional societies where collectivism is the norm, individuals have strong social bonding. India and Japan are good examples. Such bonding prevents individuals from taking on risky ventures and stepping beyond traditional lines. It also provides a strong support system to individuals to cope with failure. This may seem a good thing, but it also leads individuals to seek the protection of the cocoon. Such people never have adequate exposure to the experiences of failure.

In August 2012, IMF came out with a paper investigating the effects of national culture on risk-taking in firms, using a comprehensive dataset covering 50,000 firms in 400 industries, in 51 countries. One of the key findings was that 'risk-taking is found to be higher for domestic firms in countries with low uncertainty aversion, low tolerance for hierarchical relationships, and high individualism. Domestic firms in such countries tend to take substantially more risk in industries which are more information- opaque (e.g. finance, mining, IT). Risk-taking by foreign firms is best explained by the cultural norms of their country of origin.'

4. INDIA: THE WORLD'S SUICIDE CAPITAL

Let us revisit the September 2014 WHO report, Preventing Suicide, A Global Imperative', which said India had become the suicide capital of the world, with the most deaths per second. The report cited social, economic and educational disparity, limited access to healthcare, among many other reasons. The other countries that fared badly on these parameter were North and South Korea, Guyana, Lithuania, Sri Lanka, Hungary, and Japan.

But are not India, China, Japan, Sri Lanka and the Koreas traditional societies with collectivism? Are they not risk-averse cultures which made them less prone to failure? Then why the need to kill themselves?

The remarkable report misses out on an important factor: Our cultural perspective on failure. The report fails to take note that society is failing individual as a traditional support base. Times are changing. Western individualism is taking over traditional collectivism, prompting individuals to take more risks and break out of traditional settings. They call it 'breaking free'. But with this shift, individual has unintentionally also broken away from their traditional support system, designed to cushion the impact of failure.

Early Success	Later Success
Early Failure	Later Failure

5. THE CASE OF CHILD PRODIGIES, ACHIEVERS AND PERFORMERS

Anybody can fail and does, at some point, even someone with 140 IQ. Perhaps for different reasons. But do we really care to ask, 'Hey kid, why do you think you failed?' All we do is label him a failure. Like a script in the stock market. We place our time, effort and energy on children – and we want returns. We identify some bright stocks in which we see potential. Sometimes there are good returns and sometimes we lose on our investment. That's how we treat children and people. As investments. As potential success stories. As achievers and non-performers.

Child prodigies begin with a head start. They have exceptionally high IQ for their age and excellent memory and retention skills. When plotted on a graph, we generally see their carrier graph to be exceptionally successful, one that will go only up – a guaranteed success. But is it?

1990: India fell in love with Macaulay Culkin, the cute and adorable child who appeared as Kevin in Home Alone. We met him again in the sequels and, of course, as Richie Rich. We talked of what a great actor he was and were convinced his success in life was assured. Culkin began his acting career at 4 and announced his retirement at 14. He married at 18 and separated at 20. At 24, he was arrested and imprisoned for drug possession.

I can hear you saying: 'The kid could not handle success and Culkin came from a broken family. Hollywood does bad thing to people's personal lives. There are dozens of adults who have the same life pattern. The media spoils them.'

Prof. Joan Freeman, Fellow at the British Psychological Society, meticulously tracked the lives of 210 child prodigies for 35 years. She recounts her findings in her book, *Gifted Lives: What Happens When Gifted Children Grow Up*, in which she talks in detail about 35 such cases. She discovered that only six of 210, became successful in later life. Apparently, what goes up comes down.

What is the correlation between early and continued success, or early failure and a condemned future? What are the chances a reversal can happen? We assume that life follows a straight graph when, in fact, it is a random walk. There are so many parameters that need to be right in order to achieve overall success and happiness, and any one of them may change at any time. At the same time, those parameters may change for the good and the failure may turn to success.

Life is a like a soccer game – extremely unpredictable. Early success does not guarantee a win in the second half; nor does a blank first half mean assured failure later. The only thing we can do is to keep running. The focus on the field is always shifting. Perhaps that is the reason why, like democracy, soccer is the most popular game in the world. The logical question then is: If life is like soccer, then who are we up against?' All the factors between us and the goal become our adversaries. And what is the goal? To be happy and successful.

6. WHY DO ACHIEVERS AND PROMISING CAREERS FIZZLE OUT?

The most common reason for burnout of promise is early entry into the competitive world and the over-enthusiasm of parents to make a grand entry into the record books. Those most responsible for the angst suffered by achiever kids are, ironically, their parents.

Shakuntala Devi, the Indian child prodigy who was dubbed a Human Computer, had a father who worked in a circus. When she was three, while teaching her card tricks, he discovered she was good at numbers. He quit the circus and took her on road shows to display her abilities. Road shows? Actually, this is common among parents who suddenly discover they have a wonder child. And what did the Human Computer achieve in her 83 years? She found the 23rd root of a 201-digit number, and crashed the UNIVAC 1101 computer, and got into the Guinness Book. Think of the potential that could be developed for the betterment of society. Like so many others with special skills, Shakuntala Devi was reduced to a stage performer in a glorified circus.

Proud parents traditionally showcase their wonderful children on all possible stages, pushing the poor kids to perform till they suffer burnout. The parents have higher expectations and ambitions than the child himself. If they could keep pace with him and his learning process rather than pushing him around like a performing monkey, the outcome would be different.

Being gifted in multiple fields also brings conflicts of choice. A child who is good at maths and science may also be good at music and art. The child needs guidance in utilizing his potential. There are teachers who perceive gifted children as threats, putting them in the difficult position of having to answer tough questions. Then there are the regular bullies among their peers, who feel their under par performance is due to unfair comparison with such stars.

7. THE COST OF BEING AN ACHIEVER

The pressure to keep the top position leads to burnout and achievers trap (living in constant fear of failing, to the point of paranoia). Such people stop taking risks because any risk could result in failure which would blemish their achiever image. This heightened sensitivity towards avoiding failure leads to an erosion of confidence when facing challenges; in severe cases it can result in a mental breakdown.

What is success? To win every race you run? To get A+ in every assignment? To be 'Student of the Month' every month, followed by wealth and fame in adulthood? Can we re-set the way we measure our lives without numbers and grades; without the perpetual fear of failure?

Jean Piaget, a child psychologist (and a child prodigy himself), deduced that a child's mind isn't a blank slate, but that it is constantly imagining and testing new theories about the world and how it works. He concluded that children are not less *intelligent* than adults but they think differently. A child understands what is demanded of him and tries to adjust accordingly. So, in the face of new challenges, why not do so without fearing failure. What we really need is the commitment to *learn*. Nothing else matters. Numbers do not quantify intellect nor do grades measure personality. We sort commodities into A grade apples or a B grade potatoes, but there are no X grade people.

8. *ATYCHIPHOBIA*: FEAR OF FAILURE

Have you ever felt you were holding yourself back because there was a small chance you would fail or had a panicky feeling accompanied by increased breathing, mental anxiety, headache, tightening of stomach muscles, nausea, etc? You could be suffering from a psychological problem known as *Atychiphobia* (pronounced *ay-tie-chi*phobia) – the fear of failure, Depending on the severity of the problem, you may exhibit some or all of the symptoms mentioned above. In extreme cases it can cause paralysis, mental breakdown and/or depression. The affected person takes up a zero-risk lifestyle, completely rejecting anything with any element of uncertainty, often undermining his own potential. There is no cure for *Atychiphobia.* The only treatment is counselling and changing the mental thought process.

The symptoms of this phobia are actually a protection mechanism. The mind relates the risk to some incident associated with failure that took place in the past, usually in childhood or early adulthood. This could be something like failing in an exam and facing subsequent humiliation or punishment. Unpleasant emotions become attached to failure and the mind begins to see failure as a threat and magnifies it to unrealistically high levels, going into protection mode. Any activity with an element of risk gets rejected by the mind which is always searching for the safe path.

Though *Atychiphobia* may be an extreme condition associated with some harsh experience, the important point is that *every* child is who faces the threat of failure is affected unless failure itself is handled appropriately. Every time a child is reprimanded, humiliated, shamed or punished for failing to perform, the tender brain of the child records these events. And based on the sensitivity of the child and level of punishment, it forms linkages, with fear acting as a stimulus. He then carries those painful imprints for life. This is often done in the name of discipline but it overlooks the effects of such disciplinary action on the psychology of the child.

Once this phobia develops, it is enough to ruin a person. Chances are that he will fear failure his entire life or at least in the productive phase of his life. The threats from this phobia have been much discussed and have been major reasons for the abolition of corporal punishment in schools and homes. Perhaps this failure phobia was in the minds of policy makers when they removed all the failure hurdles in academic assessment. Perhaps they swung too far to the other extreme by removing all stimuli of failure. Child rearing is a delicate balance between the intellectual, physical, social and emotional development. We need to tread carefully as imbalances may leaving lasting imprints on the minds of children. It becomes all the more important that we manage failure with caution. Failure needs to be administered like a well- calibrated drug – excess dosages can be poisonous while too little may be ineffective, resulting in more pain in future.

9. *ACHIEVEMEPHOBIA*: FEAR OF SUCCESS

Have you ever felt yourself hesitating and holding back from a decision that could propel your career forward – an opportunity that is simply awaiting your 'Yes'? You suddenly decide you are not interested and let the golden opportunity pass. Despite all your knowledge and talent, you are marked as an underachiever, a non-performer; in future you may not be offered positions of responsibility. Instead you will be identified as possessing a unique characteristic – inability to take the critical step forward.

In Asian communities, where collectivism is a dominant force and binds society, fear of failure is omnipresent. Equally evident are situations wherein individuals are afraid to break free from the group, even if it means doing well. A feeling of guilt wells up that the other members of the family/community are not doing as well. The individual is obliged to suffer with the group even though he may be intellectually and physically stronger. Emotional bonds hold him back, tying him to the fate of the group. The focus is always on the whole group, not the individual. A person many downplay his achievements and hold back on his dreams and ambitions, just to remain part of the group. He begins to believe his success will alienate him from his family and friends and actually acts *against* his own progress. He begins to fear alienation, isolation and even rejection from his group. He fears the envy and jealousy that the limelight could trigger, hurting his relationships. His attitude becomes a barrier to moving forward. He ends up rejecting his own success. It is thus a vicious cycle where the possible consequences of success creates fear in the mind of a person, thus pushing him towards failure.

Procrastination is a strong element in the fear of success. A person delays taking important decisions: beginning big projects, starting a business, being in a relationship, knows that things are stagnating but fearing to disturb the equilibrium prevailing in his life. He fears that any decision would a storm, which would be difficult to weather. So he delays and puts off decisions and deadlines.

The jury is out on whether placing greater value on relationships than on personal growth (often sacrificing personal ambitions in the larger interests of the group), is a good thing or not. But it also means that anyone *not* emotionally attached to his family or group, stands a better chance of success. We are always busy searching for the keys to success, believing them to also be the keys to happiness. There are, however, times when happiness can be reached choosing values over success. Can we call that failure?

But here is the point to consider: Is it possible that a person's success can lift the whole family, community or nation to a better level of existence? We, as a family, a society and a nation, need to encourage individuals to achieve their ambitions, even if it means separation and letting them go.

10. *METATHESIOPHOBIA*: FEAR OF CHANGE

One factor which accentuates the fear of success is the fear of change – meta-thesio-phobia. A person fears how change will impact his life and fortifies his comfort zone, avoiding or procrastinating about decisions.

The fear of change is a natural response inherent in all living beings. It is fear of the unknown. We do not know what challenges change will present before us or whether we will we be able to keep up. Like all animals, humans tend to resist change while knowing that change is inevitable and we must adapt to it. The fear of change affects our ability to adapt to new situations.

There is, however, another face to this fear – our inability to let go. The old, tried and tested ways seem comfortable, despite their deficiencies. We prefer the known devil to the new idea, person, product or system. This is an important reason why social change is difficult to bring about. People resist because it challenges the existing way of living. Accepting change is seen as an acknowledgement that the old way was not the right way, that there was something inadequate with the traditional method.

How does fear of change result in failure? We reject new opportunities. We knowingly let them pass, considering them too risky or worthless. In our minds the old way is the right way. In his book, *Third Wave*, Alvin Toffler's discusses how change happened in human society, how societies which failed to adapt, were taken over. He mentions how agrarian societies were overshadowed by the industrial age. In the information age, businesses which fail to identify new age opportunities are being wiped out.

But isn't adapting to change a survival instinct? Imagine walking on a road and a car comes speeding along. What is your response? Would you continue walking in the same direction, ignoring the car, or jump out of the way? Well, unless you wish to commit suicide your mind will perceive the threat and your natural instinct will move you away from danger. Reacting to change is similarly linked to survival and thus a natural response.

SLOW AND FAST CHANGE

To study reaction to change, scientists placed a frog in a pot of boiling water. It immediately leapt away to safety. They then placed the frog in normal water and proceeded to heat the water gradually. The frog failed to detect the changing environment.

We too, have a tendency to resist sudden change. The fear of change is rooted in the suddenness of the change and not in change itself. We do not want to give up our ways and do things differently from tomorrow morning. Sudden changes are perceived as painful, even if they promise to revolutionize our lives. There is always a degree of uncertainty associated with change and we fear this. But, allow the change to happen gradually and we may not even notice it. However, if we do not respond appropriately and adapt, we run the risk of being left behind. This shows up as an inability to cope, underperformance, frustration and failure.

11. PRECONDITIONING:SUCCESS OR FAILURE CAN BE INDUCED

In an experiment, over 100 sixth grade students were divided into two groups and given anagram problems that none of them could solve. A researcher then spoke to them about the difficult exercise. One group was told that learning is difficult and failure common, that practice would help them do better, just as practice helps in learning to ride a bike. Children in the other group were simply asked how they tried to solve the anagrams. Both groups were then given a second test. Those who was told that learning was tough and failure a normal part of the process, performed significantly better on measures of cognitive ability than the other group.

In a separate experiment, two groups of sixth graders were given a comprehension test and asked questions about how they judged their own academic competence. One group was told in advance that learning can be difficult, the other group was not. The first group not only performed better on comprehension scores, but also reported fewer feelings of incompetence.

What can we take away from these studies is that it is very important *how* we introduce a problem. Moreover, it is possible to influence minds and either boost understanding and learning or demoralizing them into accepting defeat even before they have even begun. By telling the group that failure is part of the learning process, the educator reduced their failure anxiety. By believing that there was nothing to fear if they failed, the group tried to learn more. Teachers can increase stress levels by simply the forthcoming 'exercise will be graded, so be careful'. Failure anxiety is bound to increase and their ability to approach assignments calmly, suffer.

March and April are important months in Indian schools. This is when the Central Board of Secondary Education conducts exams for classes X and XII across India. To prepare their students, schools build pressure from the beginning of the academic year. The *Boards* are projected as tough exams and this message is drilled into the students, with the result that the students develop fear of the *Boards* which affects their abilities to take the exams. Some schools try to motivate their students by holding mock exams based on the exam pattern of the *Boards*. The result is the students overcome their fear of the *Boards* and enhance their performance.

Picture yourself accompanying a child to be vaccinated. As you wait, wailing sounds come from the children going in. You feel the child with you start to tremble and then cry. What happened? The child was induced to believe a lot of pain awaited him. The best solution is to prepare him in advance for a little pain, which 'brave guys do not fear'. Courage is the keyword here. Any surprise moves to dupe him are sure to yield nasty results.

Not just students, but educators and evaluators as well, are prone to preconditioning. In a study, 30 students were randomly selected and tested. They were then presented as outperformers and educators were lead to believe these students had great potential. The perception that they were dealing with 'star material' conditioned the educators into giving extra time and attention to the group. After three months, the group was tested again and they did much better than before. The mere conditioning of teachers resulted in improvement.

In a similar study, 30 randomly selected students were presented as under-performers. The educators slowed their pace of teaching and devoted less time. When this group was tested, their performance had either not shown any improvement or even decreased.

Why we fail or succeed is also due to the preconditioning and perceptions of our educators. If they perceive students are capable of learning more, they dispense education more actively, devoting greater time and effort. However, when they feel students are slow learner, they adapt their pace accordingly and show less interest. The teacher slows or enhances his efforts according to his own perception or the feedback he receives.

12. UNDER-ACHIEVERS: LIVING A SUB-OPTIMAL LIFE

What does sub-optimal living mean? It means living below your true potential and settling for less than what you want. Compromising and withholding. It means doing what *can* be done rather than what you *want* to do. Often, a lack of resources or opportunities, or perhaps family commitments or society pressures, creates mental and emotional strictures which restrain you. Sub-optimal living means giving in to circumstances and deciding in favour of the status quo.

Bringing out the best in individuals was never the objective of society. Communities have one objective: to survive. 'Stick Together-Stay Together-Survive' has been the motto societies have followed since the human hunter years. Nothing much has changed in this basic scheme of things. It was and is about survival.

So why do we live sub-optimally? We believe we have chosen our path when, in fact, we have been conditioned to follow the norms of the society we live in. We consciously accept and justify them or are forced to accept them. Is living an un-fulfilled life below your potential the same as failure? Who are under-achievers anyway? A person who does not perform as well as expected for whatever reasons is believed to be an under-performer.

We can draw three conclusions from this statement.

- Achievement or performance is based on our *expectations* of how well a person should do.
- The terms 'achiever' and 'under-achiever' are relative. Any grading/labelling of individuals is based on performance in relation to others in a group.
- If a group of only achievers is evaluated, there would be some who do better than others. Do we then label the latter under-achievers? Obviously not. The 'under-achievers' of this segment would be way ahead of those at the other end of the curve.

THE BELL CURVE OF PERFORMANCE DISTRIBUTION

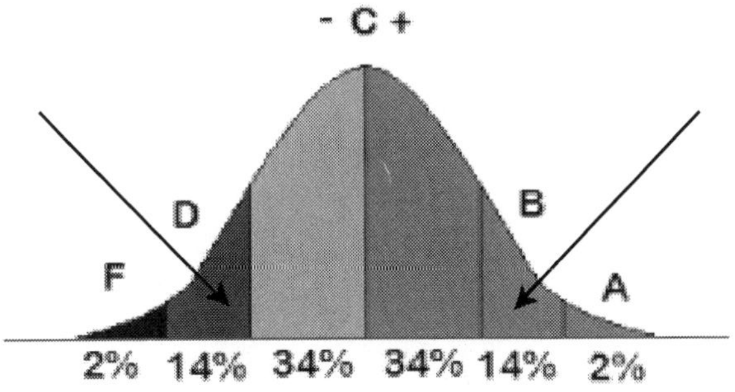

'I was considered by all my masters and my father, a very ordinary boy, rather below the common standard of intellect, wrote Charles Darwin in his autobiography. Thomas Edison, according to his teachers, was 'too stupid to learn anything'. One of Albert Einstein's teachers described him as 'mentally slow, unsociable, and adrift forever in foolish dreams'. The world is full of such under-achievers who form 2% of the Bell Curve.

Unfortunately, not everyone can journey from one end of the Bell Curve to the other. In fact, most people who are branded as under-achievers find it a major bias to overcome. The label sticks to them, causing emotional and psychological trauma, placing them at a clear disadvantage. This is compounded, often exponentially, at every stage of development, pushing the person into a downward spiral. In collective cultures such as in India, the branding also carries social stigma for both the individual and his family. The person has to fight discontent at home, the workplace and in society, making life a tough road.

13. THE HIDDEN FACE OF SUCCESS

Heroes are often presented in profile, with their best side on display. This implies there is another side to them which remains hidden and may not be as appealing.

Raja Ranjit Singh, a great ruler of Punjab, was fond of having his portrait painted. He invited famous painters from all over the world. Each one attempted to draw the king on canvas but the king was not happy. There was one problem - he was blind in one eye, and no artist could disguise this. One day, an artist from Persia approached him. He painted the king hunting in a forest. The painter showed his genius by depicting the king with bowstring drawn, the bad eye closed while the good eye took aim. The artist became the royal portrait painter.

That's the way we are. We try to hide the bad eye. But the real artist reverses the situation and glorifies it.

Success comes to those who are resourceful. But what does resourcefulness mean? It does *not* mean possessing resources. Resourcefulness is the ability to get things done by any means, fair or foul. It underlies the passion for success. But at any cost? What of those who lack resources, or those who refuse success *at any cost*; those who will not compromise their values or ethics to gain success? Not very long ago, this was the norm in Indian society. Unfortunately, a sea change has occurred and today we call people who let opportunity pass, fools or failures. The lives of failures are never written about and they are mentioned only to demonstrate how they messed up and failed to capitalize on opportunity.

14. DARK TRIAD: THE DARK SIDE OF SUCCESS II

Psychologists have identified three personality types among successful people. They call it the Dark Triad - Machiavellianism, Narcissism and Psychopathy.

Machiavellianism or the *Machs,* are manipulators. They will go to any extent to push their agenda. They have no qualms in exploiting or lying and have their own version of morality.

Narcissists are the Self-Lovers. Remember the Greek hero who fell in love with his own reflection? That's what Narcissists are -obsessed with their image. They will use any trick to be at the centre of attention, appearing charming and enthusiastic. In the long run, since they see only their own viewpoint, their decisions become difficult for others to handle. People soon realize that whatever decisions they take, serve only one purpose - enhancement of their self- image.

Psychopaths are bold, assertive, mean, and cold hearted. They believe in their own superiority and have a tendency towards self-promotion. The definitive marker of psychopathy is a lack of self-conscious emotion, guilt and conscience.

We think of successful people as our role models. But if we look deeper, we may shudder at what we might become. The cost of success is perhaps too heavy to be paid. Do we really want it? Another thought follows: Success is dangerous and difficult to handle. Fear of success raises a mental barrier which causes us to under-perform. It pulls us back from the top job. Suppose you are in line to be appointed General Manager, but the job requires you to travel and socialize. You have seen your boss become an alcoholic and the socializing affect his family life. More importantly, has had to juggle the balance sheet to show profits and give bribes to officials to get orders. You fear your life will change once you accept the position. You see yourself doing things that will challenge your moral and ethical beliefs. The top job, which once seemed so desirable, suddenly loses its charm. Fear of what you will become clouds your mind and you pass on the promotion.

I once met a magician who performed stage shows. He had gained considerable success and I was impressed by his act. So I asked him about his success story. He replied: "When I am performing on stage, I revel in the applause. Some people even believe I perform miracles. In my heart I know it is all a trick, simply sleight of hand, an illusion, fake, yet I love to keep up the act. It has become my identity."

Sometimes success is like that. We keep up the fake act because it has become who we are.

15. HOLLOW SUCCESS

Consider another list: Marilyn Monroe, Guru Dutt, Whitney Houston, Nafisa Joseph, Robin Williams Jiah Khan, Man Mohan Desai, Philip Hoffman.

- ✓ All of them were well known celebrities.
- ✓ All of them enjoyed success.
- ✓ All of them committed suicide.

Taking the extreme step is generally believed to be the reaction of people who have failed. But the case of actor Robin Williams, the Oscar winner, has cast more light on successful people committing suicide. Of course, not every successful actor or performer jumps off balconies or finds new ways to get killed, but success does take a toll. The pressure to succeed every time and portray a happy life in public becomes a burden for the glitterati.

Why do people who are at the top of their careers decide to end their lives? Researchers at the Norwegian Institute of Public Health interviewed the relatives and friends of ten young men who, despite being accomplished and successful, took their own lives. The main findings suggested they had compensated for their lack of self-worth by exaggerating the importance of their success, thus developing a fragile, achievement-based self-esteem, which left them vulnerable to rejection. They used their success to gain social popularity. They believed that if they failed, even once, they would lose their social standing and be rejected as failures. The mere thought pushed them over the brink.

16. WHAT DOES SUCCESS DO TO US?

Success is both a shield and a weapon. We use it to defend our image as well as attack the world with. This shield feeds on success and any failure is seen as a threat. We want the shield to be strong and so we put up our guard at the slightest hint of failure. Successful people want to be seen as perpetually successful. They carefully select winnable but mediocre projects, shunning creative ideas because of the risk of failure that comes attached to such projects. The stigma of failure is too much for them. Behind the sturdy shield, the person may be vulnerable due to his own lack of self worth and can be knocked down in the next storm.

We are under constant pressure to be the perfect partner, parent, sibling, friend, executive and patriot. Somewhere along the way, while playing these 'perfect' roles, we forget the individual seeking happiness, even in a state of imperfection.

17. HOPE. EXPECTATIONS. FAILURE.

Expectations and hope have strong associations with failure. While the positively associated with them can be used to counter the effects of failure, their negative avatars can magnify them, causing more harm.

Expectation is linked to something happening in the future, which is formalized in the mind. Expectations are based on data and known facts: 'I expect to get A+ in Maths' or 'I expect stocks to move up because the economy is recovering'. Expectations have a tone of certainty. If anything goes wrong and things do not work out, that would be *unexpected.*

Hope, on the other hand, is more of a wish. Hope takes into account numerous uncertainties before the final outcome. 'I hope India wins the cricket World Cup'. If I said, 'I expect India to win', I would need facts to back up the statement. Expectations are more on the lines of forecasting results. It is entirely different from hoping. No one questions hope. Nor am I expected to back it up. Hoping is personal. Everyone has the right to hope.

18. FALSE EXPECTATIONS AND FALSE HOPES

Success is as dangerous as failure. Hope is as hollow as fear.
~ Tao Te Ching

Hope is the wonder drug for the pain of failure. Hope, undeniably, is the greatest motivator in those turbulent times. It can really lift the sagging spirit. But, like all drugs, hope too, can have side effects. Lao Tzu or *Laozi*, known as the *Old Master*, was a record keeper at court in the 6th century BCE, during the Chinese Zhou dynasty. He had the opportunity to observe the ups and downs of the kingdom and the life of royalty at close quarters. His wisdom is compiled in his work, *Tao Te Ching*. The translation by the American poet and anthologist Stephen Mitchell, is perhaps the widely read.

False expectations mean I have got my facts wrong and *therefore* the expectations are wrong. I expect someone to react to a situation based on his previous behaviour or social norms. But he may decide to break those norms and displaying un-expected behaviour. What if I judged him incorrectly? False expectations arise when a person follows his own pattern while his partner expects something else. A husband, for example, may buy a piece of jewellery for his wife, expecting her to be happy when, in fact, the wife would have been happier spending some quiet time with him. The source of happiness is different for different people.

False hope is holding onto a positive scenario when the possibility of it happening is bleak or non-existent. What is more damaging – false expectation or false hope?

19. HOW HOPE WORKS

Hope is like a drug and the effect of all drugs is temporary. Hope can provide relief from the pain of failure for a limited period. But while the effects of hope *are* active, great things are possible. The person can be motivated to get out of a depressed state into action mode. Usually, the therapy of hope works well. The person experiences a small success and builds on it. By the time the effects of the hope drug wears off, the recovery from the failure has occurred. Essentially, hope provides motivation for a period, allowing the person to recover.

The wonderful thing about hope is that we start by believing in it. This perhaps is the most potent quality of hope. The line between expectation and hope vanishes and we expect that our hopes will be realized. But what if the success we have been hoping for does not happen and the effects of the hope drug wear off too soon? A deeper, far more serious crisis may well be in store, likely to cause more pain and it may be difficult to recover from. Hope is essential and works for a period of time, but it has its own limitations. It is difficult to lead a whole life on hope alone, facing repeated painful episodes. Repeated failures while in hope mode can turn hope into false hope.

False hope is not about dreaming big or having high hopes. Dreams are the foundations of hope; we do not differentiate between do- able and unachievable objectives while hoping. Nor do we tone down our dreams following failure. False hope is clinging to an impossible scenario knowing it is not going to work out. It is, in fact, a failure of hope. The very strengths that make hope an essential quality, becomes unnecessary baggage requiring disposal. Undoubtedly, hope is a wonderful thing and often proves to be the only thing keeping a person above water. But failed hope is potent enough to kill someone.

Should we then hope with caution, have realistic hopes, or not hope at all? It is difficult to draw a line between what is realistic and what is not. Hope is a wish. It does not have boundaries. We hope for a happy long life for our dear ones. We hope that all facets will align harmoniously for this to happen. At the same time we know we have little control in making it happen. But still we hope.

And if there is a choice between false hope and no hope, I would always go with false hope, knowing it may not happen. There is an element of possibility in false hope that keeps life going but with no hope, we lose everything.

So, hope is better than false hope, and false hope is better than no hope. As long as there is hope there will be some action, and as long as there is action, there is a possibility of success.

20. THE COMPLEXITIES OF CHOICE

Julu Province, China, 208 BCE: A *decisive war is fought between the ruling Qin and the insurgent Chu dynasties. The Qin forces are led by Zhang Han, while Xiang Yu leads the rebels. As war wages, another rebel state, Zhao, is placed under siege by Wang Li, a deputy of Zhang Han. The*

Zhao state sends out a call for help and Xiang Yu personally leads an army across the Yellow river. By the time he arrives, the Zhao forces in Julu are near starvation.

Xiang Yu orders his men to burn the boats they have used to cross the river. They carry with them supplies for just three days and destroy the rest. Xiang Yu's troops fight nine consecutive episodes, gaining ground with every victory. Wang Li's supply lines are disrupted. The Qin army suffer a crushing defeat. Zhang Han is forced to retreat to Jiyuan.

The battle of Julu is believed to have been a turning point in Chinese history, after which the Qin dynasty declined rapidly. When Xiang Yu ordered his men to sink their boats and burn their extra rations, he closed all options but one – to fight and win in order to survive. It became a do or die situation. The option of retreat no longer existed.

Choice can be liberating. The freedom to choose from a variety of options is like having a banquet laid out in front of you. If having options is liberating, selecting options to customize a new product is bliss. But choice can be a double-edged sword. Having too many options can result in confusion or too much time spent in decision-making. Often, too many choices cause more harm than good and becomes an important factor behind failure. Sometimes having no choice or eliminating other choices, works in our favour.

Linux offers greater choice to its users but it has not been able to displace Windows. Linux had many options while Microsoft Windows came with a set of default options. For a beginner, the exercise of choosing was a daunting task. Users found comfort in having default choices.

21. BURNING BRIDGES TO ELIMINATE CHOICE

Burning bridges means closing our options, leaving no scope for a rethink. The idea has been captured repeatedly in historical events such as crossing of the Rubicon by Alexander, after which he had no choice but to win or be executed by the Roman Senate.

What does burning bridges mean in the real world?

- Understanding what you want.
- Understanding there is no giving up or turning back.
- Closing your other options.
- Putting all your resources (effort, thoughts, emotions, passion, time and money) into your chosen area.

Closing the door to all other options requires careful thought. It is very much alike Xiang Yu asking his men to sink the boats and burn the rations or Alexander crossing the Rubicon. When there is no turning back, one has to be prepared for the repercussions.

Keeping options open is a focus-changing mechanism: 'Let me try. If I fail, I can make changes.' It is *not* Plan B – which focuses on a change of strategy while retaining the objective. Xiang Yu used different strategies when engaging the enemy nine times in the Battle of Julu. Keeping options open is about *changing objectives*. More often than not, we are too afraid to close the door to our safe haven. We are too afraid to let go and commit ourselves to the dream we wish to pursue. We are too afraid to fail. Our minds are bogged down by thoughts of 'what if?' What if, even after putting everything into single-minded and focused action, we lose? What if we put all our eggs into the same basket and the basket breaks? What if we bet everything on a single event and it does not happen? What if Xiang Yu had lost? The fact is, but for their motivation, they would have lost.

In the real world there are always chances that we may fail. Just be sure it was a risk worth taking; that you tried honestly, with complete dedication. Consider what you *could* have done. It is possible that, had you kept your options open, you might have survived. But would it then have been an honest attempt? It is better to give your dreams whole hearted attention and fail, than to attempt something half-heartedly and fail. We will live to fight another day, with no regrets. We often compare life with battle because of the decisions we make at the turning points of our lives. Sometimes we achieve what we set out to do. At these times we should recall the words of Admiral Nelson: *Now I can do no more. We must trust to the Great Disposer of all*

Events and the Justice of our Cause. I thank God for this great opportunity of doing my Duty.

22. WHY WE FAIL TO PROGRESS: THE ORBIT THEORY

The world is divided into a series of orbits, stacked one above the other. We are born in any one. Most people spend their lives in the orbit they are born into. They may or may not be happy being there but the fact is they are stuck there by compulsion or choice. If you want to change your life, you need to jump out of the orbit you were born into and enter the one above. After spending some time there, you must make efforts to move to the next level.

We have the ability to break out but more often than not, we are unable or unwilling to make that game-changing transition to the next orbit. Why? Perhaps because we have become accustomed. The daily grind is part of our routine, even enjoyable. Breaking out brings with it the risk of losing our little comforts and we become unwilling to jump even when opportunity beckons. 'What if we fail?' we ask, and let it pass. We continue to hold onto our safe haven, held back by the fear of failure rather than being led by the prospect of success. The stops lie in our minds.

But there are those who do take the opportunity and jump, moving to higher levels in life. They are able to change not just their own life but those of everyone connected to them, eventually pulling them also to the next level.

The orbit theory was proposed by Dhirubhai Ambani, while describing his own life. He rose from being a petrol pump attendant to establishing India's largest company, Reliance Industries. He used the orbit theory to describe why some people end up leading average lives while others muster the strength to jump to the next orbit. While the masses continue to hold back in their orbits, almost all rags-to-riches stories belong to people who made that crucial jump.

But how do we move to a higher orbit? Through the choices we make or do not; the roads we take or do not. Sometimes, bound by tradition, culture, ethics or values, we may choose not to remain as we are. At other times, our traditions and values help us in making the transition. Breaking an established mindset is the biggest challenge. The risks are real. It requires courage to keep moving forward to the next orbit.

23. WHY HUMANITY FAILS: BYSTANDER APATHY

In the epic *Mahabharata*, when Draupadi is humiliated at court, no one comes to her aid. Even Bhishma, the Kuru elder statesman, Dhitarashtra, the King, and the various elders who had the authority to control the situation, remained silent. Were they all gripped by bystander apathy? The situation was finally salvaged by a third party, Krishna, who was reportedly not present.

Every day there are hit-and-run cases, public harassment of women, and even murder, committed in populated locales, when no one comes forward to help. The victim/s lie on the road, often in a pool of blood, pleading for help, but no one steps forward. It is only when we read about it in the papers or see videos of the incident, that we feel enraged and question why basic humanity failed. Why would someone shoot a video rather than step forward to help?

In northern India, there is a word – *tamashbeen* – for bystanders who gather to watch a horrific event for enjoyment. They feel elated by the excitement of the incident. 'Why were so many people just standing there, watching? Why didn't someone do something?' we ask. It seems so irrational. What do we need to bring rationality and sanity back? When there is a threat to one's life, the response to save oneself is understandable, but a host of incidents keep happening around us, which pose no threat to our lives. Yet we refrain from helping or getting involved.

Although the *tamashbeen* effect is considered a typical Indian scenario, it is, in fact, a universal human phenomenon, identified as the 'bystander effect'. The concept was identified by social psychologists, Bibb Latané and John Darley, in 1964, when a young woman, Catherine Kitty Genovese, was stabbed to death outside her apartment in New York, in broad daylight. As many as 34 witnesses, who were her neighbours or shoppers, were identified. They observed the crime but did not come forward to the help or stop the crime from happening. Nor did anyone call the police. The psychologists stated the people were not being insensitive to the young woman's plight but merely thought *someone* would take the responsibility to do what was necessary. Apparently no one did.

Latané and Darley determined that people were more likely to help a victim when they were alone, rather than as part of a crowd of witnesses, where there is a *diffusion of responsibility* and everyone feels it is a collective responsibility and so waits for someone else to react. Also, the *principle of social influence* gets triggered. Bystanders monitor the reactions of others to see if it is necessary to intervene. If the others do not react, individual bystanders do not intervene.

We simply ignore the ugly scenes enacted on our roads, in our public places and transport, and in our neighbourhoods, assuming that whatever is happening is a personal matter between the parties and none of our business. Or we wait for others to take the lead. As we wait for *someone* to do the right thing, someone may lose their life or honour. We remain apathetic. Can we, as individuals and a society, live with such a stigma? Well, we certainly have, since the age of the *Mahabharata*, waiting for a hero to take the responsibility to do the right thing.

*****

Can enactment of the Good Samaritan Law protect people from being harassed and overcome bystander apathy? People are pushing for such a law as a safety net for those who step forward to help. The authorities are sceptical, suspecting that the Samaritan is often the one who has committed the crime. The fact remains that such a law cannot in itself change culture. That is perhaps why so many laws remain on the books but have little impact on society. People in different countries react to similar laws differently. Some, like Argentina, have made it a legal offence to ignore a victim on the road, punishable by two years in prison. And yet public apathy remains. People give all sorts of reasons for not helping a victim, such as being harassed by the police, the courts, hospital staff, and even the family of the victim. But the real reason lies in basic human psychology. People simply do not want to take the responsibility of the first step. It is a matter for social psychologists rather than legislators to ponder over and solve.

*****

PART VI: TEACH FAILURE: THE NEED TO FAIL

The greatest danger for most of us is not that our aim is too high and we miss it, but that it is too low and we reach it. ~ Michelangelo

1. THOU SHALL NOT FAIL: FEAR OF THE CAPITAL RED 'F'

Failure happens in school all the time. But the capital red 'F' instils a fear of failure rather than making it into a learning experience. The years spent in school nurture the fear of failing, establishing it firmly in our minds. Our minds are thus trained to fear failure and punishment for committing mistakes. So we avoid risks. Whenever an opportunity presents itself and we have to choose between risking failure and the safe path, the latter becomes our default choice.

School is where we spend the most important time of our lives: our formative years. Outside the home, school is the most important factor in shaping our lives. This book is not anti-school; it merely suggests areas that need a rethink in terms of policy and operations. The impressions formed in childhood continue throughout our lives. Much of our adulthood is spent in un-learning what we have been taught in the protected environment of school. When we step into the outside world, we learn how the real world works. Many things need a different perspective; the way we look at failure for instance. Failure is accompanied by humiliation, punishment (mental and capital), contempt, and even isolation, to drive home the message: *Thou Shalt Not Fail.* The system works. The paranoia of fear develops. We do carry the fear of failure into adulthood, fearing everything till it becomes irrelevant. The journey to a failed life begins with the capital red 'F' in school.

The larger question is, why are schools attached to the notion of success and failure? Perhaps because the evaluation of its students determines the success of the school itself. Schools are like assembly lines which children get on for processing. The school authorities strictly maintain a quality check, weeding out the faulty ones, who would reflect on the success of the line managers. The only problem is that students are not objects. Every child is unique and requires a specific approach. The standardized process leaves no scope for individual attention. So, like bottles on an assembly line, children move from one level of maturity to another. The focus of schooling, in this assembly line approach, shifts from education to testing. The schools become centres of testing rather than centres of learning.

2. UPGRADE YOUR DREAMS; DOWNGRADE YOUR FEARS

These are not just words but essential components of the continuum called life. Dreams are the change we wish to live. But in transcribing those dreams in the real world, we are bound to make mistakes. We cannot be right the first time, every time. If we are, then we are extremely lucky. But most of us need that eraser at the other end of the pencil to put our dreams on paper. But every time we come up with a refined version of our ideas. Failure and mistakes are essential processes that help us to evolve. For that we must downgrade our fears of stumbling or falling flat on our faces.

Should we actually tell that failing is a good thing? What an absurd idea! Should we let our kids fail? Yes – in a controlled manner, with safety nets in place. Parents form the primary support system for kids.

It is therefore very important that small failures are experienced in a manner that does not threaten the child. Punishment is generally awarded as a consequence of failure. We think that by suffering (in whatever way), a child will be deterred from repeating the mistake.

We can change how we view failure – as a learning experience rather than a punishment. Suppose your child seeks your help in doing his homework but you believe he has the ability to do it himself; he is simply not utilizing his potential or he is afraid he may not deliver. So what can you do? Deny the request and offer rewards if he completes the assignment himself. There is good chance he will claim the reward. Even if he fails, the reward should still be given for having made a sincere attempt. In refusing to do his work, he might feel you are not supporting him, but sometimes have to push chicks so that they learn to fly. You will keep a watch, but obliquely. You are making your child exert himself, develop his potential and overcome his fear of failure.

Consider another short list (although it can fill up reams): 1998: Sabeer Bhatia sold Hotmail to Microsoft. 1999: Mark Andreessen sold Netscape to AOL. 2005: Steve Chen and Chad Hurley, co-founders of YouTube, sold it to Google.

The world is full of one hit wonders, known for a single success. The OHW bug has long made its presence felt in the music world. Singers with single hits are legion. But the OHW list spans literature, cinema, music, sports, science and business, even though that one success was big enough to cause a major change in their personal lives as well as in their area of expertise. Hotmail, for example, heralded the era of free email; they never repeated the grandeur of that first time success.

In the 1990s, a new order was created and youngsters, mostly in their twenties, were led the movement. They found themselves in the right place at the right time. Their stories were remarkably similar – they had a great idea, developed it, founded companies, then sold it, raking in millions. They had another idea, floated another company, and lost half their money. Again they thought of something which they considered would be a big technical breakthrough, but they failed to create their initial success. It seemed the tech kids were blessed with a one-time Midas touch.

3. WHAT CAUSES A ONE HIT WONDER (OHW)?

Most OHWs in the 1990s enjoyed uninterrupted success for a while – a dream run. Fresh out of college, they landed plum jobs in a nascent industry, hatched ideas, and that was it. Some even dropped out of college to pursue those ideas. Few of these young Turks had any meaningful encounter with failure. Once they tasted success, they sincerely believed in their genius, disregarding the significance of their being in the right place at the right time. They refused to believe they were creatures of circumstance. The OHWs of the tech world really believed they were responsible for driving growth. Having stuck gold once, they believed they possessed the Midas touch.

Since they overestimated their abilities, all caution was thrown to the winds. With no exposure to failure, most of them spent much of their newly-earned fortunes and invested heavily in their ideas. They spent large amounts in setting up plush offices, paid lavish salaries, travelled business class, and stayed in seven star hotels.

Since the OHWs also believed they possessed the golden touch, they took on huge debts, assuming that every bit was recoverable once they repeated their magic. When the tech bubble burst in 2000, Silicon Valley, the Mecca of the tech world, witnessed the bloodiest of times. For most, *this* was their first brush with failure, which also happened to be the harshest.

What do most OHWs end up doing if they survive and still have some money? They bet on other people's ideas and become venture capitalists. The positive part is that they *do* succeed in this new avatar. Why? Between their initial success and their new role, these OHWs have encountered failure and become aware of their own weaknesses. This knowledge prepares them for success.

What is failure? Something that did not work out. There is no point wasting your life over it. Do something that *will* work out. Use failure as a learning resource. Nothing ever goes to waste.

INSTITUTE OF BRILLIANT FAILURES

An initiative by ABN-AMRO, the Institute of Brilliant Failures, has been set up to promote a positive view of failure. Their statement of purpose states: *Time and time again, history has shown that our most valuable experiences are more likely to come from mistakes than from successes. We learn from our failures and our failures are a source of inspiration for others. In this respect, failure is not only an option but also necessary!*

These efforts could be wasted in a culture where failure is viewed as unacceptable and few are prepared to take the necessary risk. It is painful to hear people, even kids not yet in their teens, fretting over failure. Life is too important and too short to worry about failure. We should be happy we have taken a step to learn something. Become the First Penguin – rush to fail at something spectacular.

Randy Pausch, during his teaching career as a professor of computer science at Carnegie Mellon University, taught his students that it took courage to attempt something new and such people often face repeated failure before gaining success. In his last lecture he said: *In a virtual-reality course I taught, I encouraged students to attempt hard things and not worry about failing. At the end of the semester, I presented a stuffed penguin – The First Penguin Award –to the team that took the biggest gamble while not meeting its goals. The award came from the idea that when penguins jump into water that might have predators, well, one of them has got to be the first penguin. In essence, it was a prize for 'glorious failure'.*

Pausch compared the prize to penguins lined up on a glacier, afraid to jump into the water which may have predators waiting to feast upon them. If they stayed where they were, they would all die of starvation. Still they wait, until one brave penguin decides to jump. He is aware of the risks but still he dares to act. Encouraged, the rest follows and jumps into the water.

Since reading Pausch's last lecture, I have come across numerous versions of the First Penguin in daily life. One instance was shown on Discovery: A mother duck was leading a line of ducklings to the water. The little ones, barely out of their shells, came to a place where they needed to jump from a height. It is called 'imprint'. Although it was less than a feet off the ground, it seemed dangerous to the little ones. Every single one registered the danger and was afraid as they had not had lessons in flying. Following their mother was essential but fear of getting hurt held them back. Finally, one of the little fellows mustered enough courage and overcoming his fear, took the leap of faith while the others watched in apprehension. Once our hero had landed safely, the other chicks jumped as well. Soon, everyone had jumped and joined their mother. They continued their journey to the water.

Perhaps we should have a First Duckling Award, to honour the spirit of the brave little chick who took the first jump.

4. EDUCATION INSTITUTES VS INDUSTRIAL ORGANIZATIONS

Industrial development is associated with manufacturing and the utilization of resources. The industrial lexicon is full of terms such as efficiency, cost cutting, standardization, processes, zero defect, etc. The focus is on achieving maximum output with minimum input. The processes are designed to increase one set of objectives while minimizing the other.

Increase: Productivity, efficiency, predictability, performance, profits, resource utilization.

Decrease: Losses, labour cost, fuel cost, wastage, effort, time, expenses, defects, machine cost, errors, shutdowns, failures.

Essentially, manufacturing works on the standardization of processes, eliminating variability and thus increasing the predictability of outcomes, ensuring uniform quality. Coca Cola, for instance, wants the same can to emerge from their production line every time, millions of times. Indeed, as customers we would be surprised to receive a different can every time.

Inspired by the success of standardization in manufacturing, enthusiasts began adopting the concept in educational institutes as well. But can education and manufacturing be compared? Do we really want student factories that take in children as raw material and turn out finished products? Another set of issues, still more disturbing, crops up – wastage. In an assembly line, faulty pieces are automatically weeded out and sent for recycling. But how do we deal with children who do not measure up? Weed them out? And send them where?

Unfortunately, this is exactly what happens when children do not measure up. Instead of questioning the measuring system, we fault the children, rather like a defective can of Coca Cola. The principal objective of standardized processes is to test and measure everything so that they work correctly, eliminating human error. But educational institutes have very different objectives from the manufacturing industry – literacy, creativity, mind development, learning, responsibility, civics, knowledge, interaction, leadership, growth. When an educational institute adopts industry standards such as Six Sigma or ISO, it necessarily conforms to industry objectives and moves to increase efficiency, predictability and performance. To achieve this, frequent performance reviews are held for both students and teachers. The idea is to bring objectivity into the system.

Objectivity is not however, the right metric for educational institutes since the development of the human mind is a dynamic process. It learns *and* forgets at the same time. A cola can cannot correct or change itself. The human mind can; it works on the principle of use and disuse. Often, what is learned at the beginning of an academic year is forgotten by the end. And every child needs time and attention to develop individually, unlike cola cans that respond to the same temperature and pressure.

Another reason why objective metrics are unsuitable for measuring child development is because they do not measure half development or some development. In the manufacturing world, mistakes are failures, not to be tolerated. In the human world, however, mistakes are part of the developmental process.

5. CREATIVITY AND FAILURE ARE INTERLINKED: THE 3M LEGACY

The Minnesota Mining and Manufacturing Company was established to mine a mineral to be used as a grinding-wheel abrasive. But the deposits proved to have little value. So the company decided to make sandpaper. But then customers began complaining that the stones in the sandpaper kept falling out. The Company found the stones had absorbed oil and so failed to stick to the paper. They finally solved the problem by roasting the stones to remove the oil. Over the years, the single product company that failed initially came to be known as 3M, producing over 55,000 products, marketed in 200 countries.

William McKnight, the philosopher-CEO of 3M, wrote the management principles for the company in 1948. They continue to guide the company today: *As our business grows, it becomes increasingly necessary to delegate responsibility and to encourage men and women to exercise their initiative. This requires considerable tolerance. Those men and women, to whom we delegate authority and responsibility, if they are good people, are going to want to do their jobs in their own way. Mistakes will be made. But if a person is essentially right, the mistakes he or she makes are not as serious in the long run as the mistakes management will make if it undertakes to tell those in authority exactly how they must do their jobs. Management that is destructively critical when mistakes are made kills initiative. And it's essential that we have many people with initiative if we are to continue to grow.*

3M takes pride in preserving a culture of hiring good people and letting them do their job in their own way, tolerating mistakes.

What is the correlation between mistakes and greatness? Great people have made more mistakes than the mediocre. Innovation and failure are close associates. As innovators not everything may work out as we envisage. There are no guarantees for success.

DO YOU CELEBRATE YOUR FAILURE?

- ✓ Yes, I aimed high knowing very well that I might lose.
- ✓ Yes, I did not fail. Rather, I gained invaluable experience.
- ✓ Yes, I will use the experience to do better.
- ✓ Yes, I have advanced on my learning curve.
- ✓ It was a reality check. I now know my weakness.
- ✓ Failure has given me a new perspective on the world.
- ✓ I am more humble and appreciate the value of success.
- ✓ The experience has been a spiritual experience.
- ✓ I understand the pain of failure and can empathize more.
- ✓ I now appreciate the contribution of scientists/authors and the value of awards.

6. THE DROPOUT'S SUCCESS: FAILURE IS NOT A NOUN

How have some dropouts made it to the top? How did those whom their teachers and critics had written off with poor grades and humiliating comments, bounce to the top? Hard work? Persistence? Or just plain luck? Should we take grades and comments with a pinch of salt? Does this mean that our education system (more importantly, the evaluation system), is a failure? What kind of evaluation system fails an Einstein or rejects the Beatles? Would we be better off without such a system? Finally, the moot question is: Are dropout successes mere exceptions?

Dropping out cannot be considered a required qualification for success in life. In fact, data tells us the inverse is true. More dropouts correspond to an increase in crime rate and illegal activities. Without jobs, many turn to the parallel economy.

So how do we identify the Einsteins? Is it possible that we have lost a few to the parallel economy? Absolutely! Some of the brightest brains rule the grey economy and give the law enforcement agencies a tough time.

Undoubtedly, the evaluation system is not perfect. It is designed to spot trends. Where it fails is in identifying hidden talent. Similarly, slow learners have a tough time with evaluators, who can identify slow learners but are not trained to discover *why*. It could be family problems, confidence issues, bullying by classmates, or that he is going through a bad time.

In class V, I had a friend who was a good student. Suddenly his scores began to decline and he developed an abnormal fear of Maths. This continued for three years and he began losing interest in his studies. Then one day, he confided in me that he could not read the blackboard properly and he suffered from frequent headaches. It turned out that he had myopia and simply needed corrective glasses. By then he had lost four years of valuable formative training. The evaluators had continued to grade him on his exams, giving him lower grades without wondering why. Einstein's issue was self-confidence not talent. When a teacher asked a question, he never put up his hand, not because he didn't know the answer but because he was not sure of it. Evaluators were/are not trained to handle that.

7. GRADE INFLATION: NOTHING BUT 'A'

May-June 2014, the admission season for undergraduates in Delhi, saw an interesting trend – an overwhelming number of A-graders applied for admission. The University resorted to the highest percentages as criteria for selection. Every seat went to an A-grader. Even those on the waitlist were A-graders. History was made. The learning ability of students seemed to have broken all records. But was that the real truth?

The jubilation ended there. The other side of the story was that the B-graders never got a chance. B had become the new F. It was not only the A-s had expanded their domain but that F had taken over B, C, D and E. Effectively, there were only two grades: A and F.

The Grading scheme

A- 90%-100%
B- 80%- 90%
C- 60 %-70%
D- 50%-60%
E - 33%-50%
F- Below 33%

Ground Realty

A- 90%-100%
B- Below 90%

What did this mean? Even though it seemed like the A-s were everywhere, it was really the F band that had expanded. Students who scored 89% were forced to look for alternative education set-ups such as Open Universities, to finish their education.

Grade inflation has skewed the academic scenario. The real objective behind liberal grading was to shrink the F band but this has proved to be self-defeating. Those with B, C, D or E grades have nowhere to turn. They undergo the same mental stress as F-graders. It has compounded the problem as the number of 'average' students is much larger than the original F band. And with a glut of A-graders, A has been devalued.

There was a time, not very long ago, when 100 rupees was enough to buy a month's grocery supplies. A 100 rupee note carried value and was treated with respect. Today, it cannot get us a meal in a restaurant. Economists describe this as inflation. Stated simply, it means that money loses its worth. This is exactly what we have done with the grading system. We have distributed A-s liberally so many student hold it, but they cannot redeem it to get a good education. This is grade inflation, where the grades have lost their worth. Distributing currency notes does not decrease poverty. Similarly distributing high grades does not increase the knowledge or decrease stress among students. 'A' has been devalued.

Do grades serve any purpose? In kindergarten children are given smileys and stars when they do well. Children see such markers as motivation to keep up with their performance. Letter grades are introduced in higher classes to evaluate performance. In professional courses, even letter grades are eliminated as the transition is made to performance evaluation and competition. This measurement serves to differentiate individuals.

'One of the things we've seen from all our data crunching is that G.P.A.s are worthless as a criteria for hiring, and test scores are worthless,'says Laszlo Bock, Senior Vice People Operations, at Google. 'Successful bright people rarely experience failure, and so they don't learn how to learn from that failure. Those people have an unfortunate reaction [and] commit the fundamental attribution error, which is if something good happens, it's because I'm a genius.

If something bad happens, it's because someone's an idiot or I didn't get the resources or the market moved. ....What we've seen is that the people who are the most successful here, who we want to hire, will have a fierce position. They'll argue like hell. They'll be zealots about their point of view. But then you say: Here's a new fact, and they'll go: Oh well, that changes things; you're right.'

In an interview to the New York Times, Bock also said, 'Academic environments are artificial environments. People who succeed there are finely trained and conditioned to that environment. One of my own frustrations when I was in college and grad school is that you knew the professor was looking for a specific answer. You could figure that out, but it's much more interesting to solve problems where there isn't an obvious answer. You want people who like figuring out stuff where there is no obvious answer.'

Succeeding in academia isn't always a sign of being able to do a job. Perhaps this is the reason why top of the class don't fare well when they step out of school.

In 1492, three ships left Spanish waters to conquer the paradise that was Asia. The Commander of the ships held the firm conviction that the world was round and by sailing west they would reach eastern lands. He had charmed the Queen of Spain into funding the expedition and promised to bring back riches and fine silks from China. Following a 36-day journey, he landed on the shores of the Indies. Leaving some men to explore for gold, he returned with some natives. When he reached Spain, he proudly displayed the natives as proof. The Queen honoured him and also persuaded the King to extend royal sponsorship for further explorations.

The Commander made four journeys across the seas, establishing newer sea routes and contributing immensely to the world of navigation by linking Europe to the New World. The United States still celebrates 12th October as a Federal holiday,500 years after he touched American shores. The Commander was Christopher Columbus, and the Queen, Isabella of Spain. Columbus is perhaps the most famous sailor in history, credited with introducing Europe to the Americas. He was the first person to do trans-Atlantic journeys. His sea routes resulted in massive changes in cultivation as well, introducing potatoes to Europe, wheat to Australia, and sugarcane, coffee and rubber across regions. Without his challenging popular belief that the world was flat, there would not have been a USA as we know it today, or Canada, Australia and New Zealand.

But was he really successful? Till his dying day Columbus believed he had found new routes to Asia and the natives he brought home belonged to an island off the coast of China. Even though he opened the Americas to Europe, he actually failed in his intent. By sailing west he literally landed in the West, and not the East, as he believed he would. Modern historians are of the view that Nordic explorers beat Columbus to North America by a few hundred years; they landed on the northern part of the continent.

The real objective of Columbus' voyage was to expand the Spanish empire by establishing new colonies around the world. When he returned home from his first journey, he presented a business plan to the Queen. The natives he had brought were not, in fact, proof of his successful landing, but specimens for the slave trade the Commander proposed to establish. The Queen rejected the plan.

Columbus never found fabled riches of the East or fine China silk. Every time he journeyed forth, he had to deal with rebellious natives. Finally the Spanish army brought him back, in chains. His titles were taken away. It was left to his sons to fight for his legacy and due acclaim.

8. PERCEPTION OF SUCCESS (AND FAILURE)

One of the most important reasons behind failure is the definition of success and failure made by society. A person can be judged or complimented based on perception. There are ideas for which society is not ready and does not understand its significance. Consequently, such ideas get rejected or ignored. Then there are ideas which challenge the authority of those in power. They perceive such ideas as threats or encroachment on their turf. Consequently they put up their protective shields and respond by rejecting the idea. Then, of course, there are those who believe the ideas offer nothing new. Fortunately, somewhere someone *does* accept revolutionary ideas that keep the world going.

'I am bored, so I fail.' I have heard this from many people who have dropped out of regular streams of study. They do not find the system stimulating enough. *Eventually I came to conclude that I could not find real knowledge in academic life, only hierarchies of knowledge that led, ultimately, to more hierarchies, not to more knowledge. I began to see university learning as limited, human, and relative. What was seen as absolutely up-to-date did not consider the infinite and timeless*, said Sharon Daniels. Sometimes, dropouts happen because they are ahead of their time. But sometimes they happen because they get tangled in the web of their evaluators' egos.

Evaluators follow set guidelines to detect talent. But often, especially in the performing arts, it is a subjective evaluation. If the judge is impressed, you pass. What impresses a judge? It depends on his cultural background, education, personal exposure and experience. How do you determine what will impress a judge? You can't. The same performance can be faulted or praised, depending on the judge. Sometimes dropouts are ahead of their time and they need another platform to develop their case.

So should we dump the system? I don't think so. But its scope needs to be widened. Evaluators need to be trained to spot both rising and declining trends. A sudden decline should certainly set alarm bells ringing. Similarly, they need to discover why a child is not participating, especially if he is quiet and sensitive. Is he an introvert? How can the best be brought out in him?

Did someone train you to play video games? Did someone train you to use the fridge or mobile phone? Most of us simply learn to operate gadgets and play games. We learn the rules without a tutor telling us, simply by trial and error. So what is trial and error? Trying and

Failing, and then doing it over again, learning from every failure, *improving* with every failure. Wouldn't it have been easier to call on an expert? Absolutely. But by doing it our way, by trial and error we become more familiar and learn to troubleshoot. We become more confident. Our learning curve is longer because of the mistakes we made but we learned much more than we would have by simply listening to the expert.

Can learning from trial and error work in academic institutions, where students are normally instructed by teachers? Instead, can we turn things around and the students begin by trying out an activity by themselves and only approach the teacher when they get stuck? Just like a baby eager to walk begins his first steps without instructions from his parents, and falls.In April 2012, the Times ran a story, *Why Floundering Is Good* by Annie Murphy Paul, which said: *Trying to figure something out on your own before getting help actually produces better results than having guidance from the beginning.*

The learning paradox is 'Productive Failure', a phenomenon identified by Manu Kapur, a researcher at the Learning Sciences Lab at the National Institute of Education, Singapore. Productive failure deliberately puts students into problem-solving situations that are over their heads. Wrestling with the problem in collaboration with other students sets the brain up for deeper and more engaged subsequent learning that remains over the long term. The brainstorming also gives instructors a chance to gauge what students already know and can do.

In the real world, problems rarely come neatly packaged, so being able to discern their deeper structure is the key. Kapur notes that none of us like to fail, no matter how often Silicon Valley entrepreneurs praise the salutary effects of an idea that flops or a start-up that crashes and burns. He says we need to 'design for productive failure' by building it into the learning process. Kapur has identified three conditions that promote this kind of beneficial struggle. First, choose problems to work on that challenge but do not frustrate. Second, provide learners with opportunities to explain and elaborate on what they're doing. Third, give learners the chance to compare and contrast good and bad solutions to the problems.

But the concept is not easy to sell to parents. People don't like failure. 'Why do my kids need to fail?' they ask. But failure in a controlled environment is entirely different from what happens when a student flunks an important test, course or semester. Those failures are humiliating and the feelings of incompetence they foster can kill a person's motivation to keep trying.

9. THE CURSE OF THE PERFECTIONIST

Next time you meet someone who appears to be brilliant but has little to show for it, don't rush to label him an underperformer or failure. You may be dealing with a perfectionist. Handle him carefully; you may have a winner.

'Perfection or Nothing' is a motto celebrated by leaders and motivators. The fact is that more often than not, you end up with nothing. Every idea, invention or system created by man has evolved over many years. It is the result of many minds working to eliminate imperfections. We have yet to see something which does not have flaws. *Perfectionism drives people to attempt to achieve an unattainable ideal and can sometimes motivate them to reach their goals. In the end, they derive pleasure from doing so. When perfectionists do not reach their goals, they often fall into depression.Perfection is not attainable. But if we chase perfection, we can catch excellence*, wrote Vince Lombardi.

Then why have such lofty ideals if they are unachievable? The answer lies within the question. Perfection can never be achieved but we can *strive* towards it.*Understanding the difference between healthy striving and perfectionism is critical to laying down the shield and picking up your life. Research shows that perfectionism hampers success. In fact, it's often the path to depression, anxiety, addiction, and life paralysis*, says Brené Brown in her book, *The Gifts of Imperfection.*

Does that mean we need to promote mediocrity and sloppy work? Absolutely not! All we need to do is define the scope of work, present it, get feedback and let other minds work on it also. Some of the best minds have faced failure because they wanted to create the perfect invention, the perfect painting or the perfect research. They were through 90%, but just could not get that final 10%. They did not have the courage to present to the world their 'half-cooked' wonders and so suffered the pain of failure. It is almost certain that had they floated their ideas and initial work, others would have contributed to developing it. Many marriages fail because we want a perfect spouse. We all have our flaws which, in fact, make our identities special.

If Bill Gates had waited for the perfect Windows operating system before launching it in 1985, he would still be writing code. Instead, he had the wisdom to present it to the world and then come out with different versions, ironing out the imperfections. Considering how Microsoft Windows has revolutionized the way we use computers, imagine our loss if we were still living with DOS.

Then there is the case of Shri Aurobindo, who began writing *Savitri*, his epic poem, when he was18 years old. He was fascinated by the subject but was never satisfied with his work. He revised it 18 times over 50 years, sometimes re-writing entire sections. As his eyesight failed, he dictated the corrections to a disciple. Till the end, Aurobindo thought that there was still scope for improvement and could not bring himself to publish it. Today, *Savitri* is accepted as a masterpiece but it remained unfinished after 18 revisions and 50 years. That is the cost of perfectionism.

There are many students who strive to master the whole syllabus before an exam, always afraid of missing something important. Research shows that most perfectionists were raised being praised for achievement and performance (grades, manners, rule-following, people-pleasing, appearance, sports). Somewhere along the way, they adopted the dangerous and debilitating belief system: I am what I accomplish and how well. Healthy striving is self-focused – *How can I improve?* Perfectionism is other-focused – *What will they think?*

A request for feedback from Finn student, Linus Trovalds, set the ball rolling for another revolution in information technology – the Linux operating system: *Hello everybody out there using minix*

*- I'm doing a (free) operating system (just a hobby, won't be big and professional like gnu) for 386(486) AT clones. This has been brewing since April, and is starting to get ready. I'd like any feedback on things people like/dislike in minix, as my OS resembles it somewhat (same physical layout of the file-system (due to practical reasons) among other things).*Thousands of programmers and researchers contributed to its development and since the code was free, anyone could use it. Linux appeared in many forms. Some survived while others did not. After a while Linux re-appeared in a different avatar as the Android. It gained the patronage of Google and to date dominates the mobile operating system space.

Did Linus started out as a revolution? No. It just happened. How? The main factor was the GNU project and the people associated with it. But what if Linus had kept the project to himself, working to perfect it? He would probably still be working on it. The lesson here is: Good is good enough. Start with good. Then go on to better it. If you are stuck up, seek help. Accept suggestions. Don't wait for perfection. It may never come. Have reasonable targets. Build on small successes and enjoy them.

So who were some famous perfectionists who failed? The problem is that failures do not get written about. History loves to remember successful people. Perfectionists who failed are not enthusiastic about writing about themselves, not wanting to be remembered as one who failed. They slip into depression and just fade away, remembering painfully how close they were to success and how life could have been so different.

10. ENLIGHTENMENT THROUGH FAILURE

- Failure is a reality check. It brings us back to the ground. Failure shows us we are not invincible. Success brings euphoria. A series of successes in the early stages can even be dangerous, for it builds a sense of invincibility.

- *Experience is what you get when you didn't get what you wanted. And experience is often the most valuable thing you have to offer,* wrote Randy Pausch in *The Last Lecture*. Indeed.
- It makes us compassionate. Someone who has experienced the pain of failure becomes more sensitive towards the failings of others.
- It makes us humble. Accepting defeat takes a lot of courage. Failure helps us to accept that we were wrong. Often, failure changes our perspective on life as we begin to view the world (and ourselves) differently.
- Failure helps us understand the importance of success. It makes us appreciate the achievements of others. As we experience the pain we wonder at the resilience of those who bounced back.
- Failure exposes the chinks in our armour, showing up our weaknesses and what we need to improve.
- It forces us to think of Plan B and to accept that everything does not go like clockwork. There is no straight path to success. There are roadblocks around which you need a detour. Failure makes us think: So this failed. Now what?

II. BEING STREET SMART

With washing machines becoming ubiquitous and economical, washermen no longer wash clothes, they simply iron the ones that have been machine washed. We continue to call them washermen but it would be more accurate to say ironing-man or press-man. I once had a conversation with a University professor about this. We saw a washerman's son on the road. Just as he was about to pick up his load, a school bus came by and a group of weary kids were dropped off. The Professor remarked: 'The washerman has more chance of survival on Delhi's streets than those school kids.' 'Sure,' I replied, 'but how far can he go without education? The school kids will get lessons in being street smart in due course but will the washerman's son ever complete his schooling? Society cannot simply survive, it has to progress and evolve.'

Being street smart is essential for combating failure. It generates the necessary confidence and judgement to take on anything. But it cannot be a substitute for schooling. Education and street smartness, with exposure to failure, can be a great formula for success. In fact, most rags-to-riches stories feature this combination of street smartness and education. When Mark Twain said, 'I have never let school interfere with my education,' he was perhaps referring to the street smartness he had acquired doing various jobs in early youth. Perhaps we too, can take a cue from him and introduce a course in learning the fundamentals of being street smart, to deliver the missing punch in school education.

12. THE RAT RACE

To many people, including myself, the term 'rat race' conjured up images of rats falling over one another in their rush to get ahead. It symbolized the tough competition to get ahead in life. If one is not running or fighting, one is out of the race. It was only much later that I understood the real meaning of the term. Rat Race refers to lab rats running through mazes set up by scientists to study their behaviour. At the end of an exhausting run, the rats would be given a piece of cheese as a reward. Since they didn't perform any useful work, the term came to mean pursuing something pointless. So 'rat race' refers not to competition but to *pursuit itself*.

The obituary of the rat could then read: This rat died pursuing endless, self-defeating and pointless pursuits. All his life he ran and became hugely successful at running. Sometimes he faltered but picked himself up smartly and resumed his running. He was a rat of action and when the end came, he was still running with all his might. May he rest in peace.

What has the rat race got to do with failure? Nothing directly, but it does have to do with the perception of success. We are constantly running. Some fail and fall while others continue to run. The only objective is to keep running and remain in the race. Rarely do we pause to think what exactly we hope to achieve. Rather, we do not think because the moving wheel simply does not allow moments of introspection. The only time when it is possible to sit down and think is when we are thrown off the spinning wheel, only then can we compose our thoughts and think of the merits of running around and ask ourselves: *Is all this running worth it? Is there life outside the wheel?* But for that we need to stop running, be thrown out and fail. Are we ready for that?

13. CREATIVITY DRIVEN BY CHALLENGE

Are we driven by challenge or failure? Challenges may drive us to success or failure, but they certainly work as road blocks we must negotiate. How we react to them is a matter of attitude and culture. Attitude, because it is something an individual develops from his experiences of life, and culture because society gives it to him in the form of his upbringing. Challenges force us to think of ways to get past them. They compel us to explore alternatives to move through, around, above or below. Challenges trigger creativity.

Do successful people chase challenges? This is contrary to the popular belief that humans are hard wired to avoid challenging situations. The truth is that people who succeed *do* find ways to overcome the challenges that come their way.

The human mind, like electricity, follows a path of least resistance. It calls upon the creative side only when it is needs to. That *need* presents itself in the form of challenges. Why are we like this? Challenges are like threats and our minds perceive them as such. From earliest times, when man lived and survived as hunters, threat-perception developed as a life-saving ability. Our basic instinct says 'avoid trouble' and the mind reacts to jump out of harm's way. In the modern world, trouble includes challenges, with the mind retaining its conditioning.

We hear of diligent business people doing a risk-benefit analysis before beginning a project. The risks are simply challenges that may crop up. By identifying challenging situations the person is more likely to choose the path of least resistance. No challenge is chosen over challenge. Unless, of course, he concludes that there is no other alternative. It is only then that he shakes up his creative brain which has been lying asleep. The corporate world is forever in search of situations of least competition. But what happens when there is strong competition? Corporates find competition unnerving and search for ways to *kill* it. It is nothing short of war, using mergers, takeovers and dirty games. *No successful organization or individual, barring James Bond, goes looking for challenging situations.*

CHALLENGE AS A CREATIVE ENGINE

The surest way to get the creative juices flowing is by introducing challenges into the daily routine. Challenges small enough to force the brain to sit up and think and important enough to simulate failure, yet not so great as to generate a fear of failing which would be a temptation to abandon the task itself as un-doable.

Science, for all the halo around it, is really a race where scientists compete, using every trick to be first – first to publish research, first to register a discovery, design or innovation. The biggest symbol of this race is the patent. There are many instances of scientists working independently or in teams, competing to reach the patent office. Many dreams have been shattered and years of research left unacclaimed because of a missed patent. Cut-throat competition in the scientific world has resulted in well meaning scientists fiercely guarding their research. Such is their paranoia that they spend more time hiding or camouflaging their activity than in doing actual research. They know that to come in second is the same as failure.

Such is our obsession with originality that we have created an environment of mistrust. No scientist is willing to share his ideas and theories with others. Competition and the race has to be first overshadowed the spirit of science. Perhaps this is one of the reasons humankind has not been able to produce a blueprint for the future. All the technological breakthroughs we see today are based on the work of scientists who lived at least 100 years ago. Today, if a scientist has an idea, he keeps it locked in his desk or in his mind, depending on his level of paranoia. He keeps it locked away for years, even decades, till he finds a way to capitalise on it. In certain cases, it travels to the grave with him.

14. SCHOOLING. LITERACY. EDUCATION. SUCCESS.

Why do we have schools? We believe this is where children can learn the formula of success. These are centers where knowledge is transferred to children, where they become literate, educated, and finally, attain success. But do we really have a formula for success? And is success really a *nirvana*-like state into which we enter and remain? What is the association between schooling and success? What is success anyway? As a writer, sorting my material and to putting it down in a Word document, gives me satisfaction and a sense of achievement. To me, this feeling of happiness is success. When the material is published and commented upon by readers, it supplements that success. Thus, for every individual, pursuing different interests, success has a different meaning.

Literacy is a subjective term. A person's literacy is limited to his understanding of a particular subject. That is why we have sub-generic terms like computer literacy, financial literacy, legal literacy or technical literacy. We can have a computer in front of us but be unable to operate it. It is the same for an illiterate person handling a book. A medical doctor may know nothing about what lies under the hood of his car or what makes the ECG machine work – because he is technically illiterate. A car mechanic can tell what's wrong with a car just by the sound of its engine and yet, may not know how to read.

There is a story about Henry Ford. He was having some trouble with the assembly line at his auto factory. Ford asked his chief mechanic, Nikola Tesla, to look into the matter. Tesla walked up to the line, picked up a piece of chalk and made a small X on the part he believed to be holding up production. It was an inexpensive part and was promptly replaced. The line got moving again. Impressed, Henry Ford asked Tesla how much he owed him. '$10,000,' replied Tesla. 'Isn't that too much? After all, it was less than a half hour job and all you did was mark an X?' Ford asked. 'You're right. I am charging 1 dollar for putting the X mark; the rest is for knowing where to put the X.'

The story has many versions. In its generic form, the millionaire is a symbol of formal literacy, which the world recognizes and values. The mechanic represents the differently literate, equally essential but less valued by society. The millionaire *needs* the mechanic to run his empire but does not accord him the status due to him or equate his literacy with that of a mechanic. Therefore he undervalues the mechanic's literacy and experience.

Many illiterate people or those with basic schooling have attained cult status. It is incorrect to call them illiterate, they are simply differently literate. Sports, music, acting, dancing, singing, art, sculpting, poetry and writing all demand different kinds of literacy from what we see in schools. There are businessmen and politicians who have used their understanding of human behaviour to influence society.

Some children may be disinterested in regular school because of their different interests, while others may have genuine problems in learning. Tom Cruise suffered from childhood dyslexia and described himself as 'functionally illiterate' when he graduated from school. He found school boring and frustrating. Joining him on the list of children suffering from the reading disorder are Pablo Picasso (who often became violent at the thought of going to school as no one understood him), Albert Einstein and Steve Jobs.

It is in the areas where technical skills are required, like the sciences, that school education really makes a difference. But even then, great scientists and inventors with minimal education, such as Thomas Edison and Michael Faraday, have contributed so much to society. There are also numerous cases of educated people working for businesses established by semi-literates and dropouts.

Does that mean school is a waste of time? Absolutely not. If literacy means initiation to a subject, then school education gets us going in a number of subjects. School makes us literate in science, mathematics and social science. This is a major contribution. It just means that life exists outside formal schooling. If one does not do well in school, there is no need to get disheartened. There are loads of possibilities where one can excel and make a mark. There is an urgent need to develop alternate literacy among children, especially those who show special interest in such areas early in life.

Everybody is a genius. But if you judge a fish by its ability to climb a tree, it will live its whole life believing that it is stupid. Albert Einstein captures the essence of this discussion in this wise nugget. It is the duty of society, parents, teachers and social groups, to identify the genius of a child and help him major in it.

15. REFINING INTELLIGENCE

Our understanding of intelligence is the principle reason behind failure. Most of us live with the notion that there is only one kind of intelligence (how many can there possibly be?), and that we are born with it (either we have it or we do not). Howard Gardner, an American psychologist, in his book *Frames of Mind: The Theory of Multiple Intelligences*, differentiates intelligence into eight parts, like white light being split into seven different colours. The colours were there for us to see individually, but we never thought of them as components of the white light.

Musical-rhythmic and harmonic: These people have musical ability. They can sing, play instruments and compose music. They are sensitive to rhythm, pitch, meter, tone, melody and timbre.

Visual-spatial:This area deals with spatial judgement and the ability to visualize with the mind's eye. Spatial ability is one of the three factors in the hierarchical model of intelligence.

Verbal-linguistic: They are the wordsmiths, good at reading, writing, telling stories and memorizing words and dates.

Logical-mathematical: The mathematicians of the world, they are good at logic, abstractions, reasoning, numbers and critical thinking.

Bodily-kinaesthetic: They are dancers, gymnasts, sportspersons and even army men. This intelligence involves excellent control over body movements and ability to train their responses.

Inter-personal: Those with social skills. Inter-personal intelligence is often misunderstood as being extroverted or liking other people. Individuals with high inter-personal intelligence are more sensitive to others' moods and feelings and show empathy.

Intra-personal: This area has to do with introspective and self-reflective capacities. It refers to a deep understanding of the self, one's strengths and weaknesses, what makes one unique and being able to predict one's own reactions/emotions.

Naturalistic: People with a deep-rooted interest in nature. This was a survival resource during the early stages of evolution when human were hunters, gatherers, and farmers. Today, the ability is found in ecologists, environmentalists and biologists.

Existential: Those with existential intelligence to understand man's spiritual journey and the greater Universe.

This new understanding of intelligence enables us to view people with different capacities in their own light. This enabling perspective becomes crucial when dealing with children. While we are measuring their academic performance, it is possible they are be exhibiting a different form of intelligence, which goes un-noticed - an ear for music or a liking for dance or sports. This could be the reason why many celebrities failed miserably in school. The fact is that they shone not because of the system but *in spite* of it. To put aside the scars of failure from their tender years in order to bring out their positive best, was a tough and challenging task. That they succeeded pays tribute to their ability and their endurance.

Can we devise a system where intelligence can be identified and nurtured in the early stages of development? And once identified, can we enhance its potential? Our understanding of intelligence is the primary reason we teach our children the way we do. It is also the reason why many fail. If we can set up different methods and approaches for honing different intelligences, it would cut down the failure rate and result in a more inclusive society.

PART VII: MANAGING FAILURE

Failure does not mean you have failed.
It means you have not succeeded yet.
~ Robert Schuller

1. HITTING THE WALL

What do we do when, after trying repeatedly, we still hit the failure wall? *Realize the power of failure.* The first step in managing failure is to recognize its true nature. Failure is a powerful force. It has the potential to cause anxiety, depression and even death. But if we can harness that power to our advantage, it can be a motivating force capable of transforming our lives.

Maintain a relationship with failure and shed Failure Phobia. To harness the power of failure, we must maintain a harmonious relationship with it. But as long a Failure Phobia persists, we will try to keep it away. We will avoid taking risks so as to minimize our chances of failure and thereby block our minds to a vast window of opportunity.

It is important to develop tolerance to failure – the ability to accept failure and use it as feedback to move forward. How does it help?

It encourages risk-taking associated with innovation and novel methods. More importantly once failure is understood as an input in our development, we will not be tempted to brush it under the carpet. Failure inputs are, in fact, evolutionary inputs to success. Thus, developing tolerance to failure reduces risk-taking phobia, encourages initiative, and finally helps us to reach our objective.

2. WHAT TOLERATING FAILURE DOES NOT MEAN

For one, it does *not* mean lowering the standards bar. There must be zero tolerance towards shoddiness and sloppiness. When Edison found that thousands of his experiments yielded nothing, he elaborated on the procedures for *each* one. Every material was tested. He also devised and maintained detailed records and notes.

The idea behind failure tolerance must be understood clearly. It does *not* mean pushing people and systems into failure. It also does *not* mean compromising on standard operative procedures (SOPs) that every industry adopts for its functioning. Nobody wants trains and planes crashing because someone failed to perform routine checks. We still feel the pain of space shuttle Challenger exploding in mid-air. The disturbing fact remains that the failure of the mission was caused by a tiny, faulty component that escaped detection.

We also need to appreciate the difference between failing and not succeeding. Failing implies taking some action but not getting the desired results, whereas not succeeding does not imply action. We may take no action and let an opportunity pass, and then claim to have been unsuccessful. In fact, letting the opportunity pass qualifies as failure.

Failure is an event not a person – a fundamental and powerful quote from Zig Ziglar. We must distinguish between the person and the event. Events happen; they have an outcome. People take part in an event and continue, no matter what the outcome. Whatever we may say about learning from failure and fighting it out, the reality is that sometimes failure is more persistent than we are. We may be strong and do our best, but it is just does not seem good enough.

We ask our children: 'What do you want to be when you grow up?'Expectedly, the replies are our common role models – doctors, engineers, rock artists, painters, actors, and so on. Sometimes they succeed in their wishes, and sometimes they don't. When they don't, they engage in alternative occupations and often lead dissatisfied lives, grumbling about their failure. Closure never comes. The hurt never goes away. They continue to dream of a life that could have been. Sometimes they push their children towards their own unfinished dreams. When the child has own dreams, it can result in conflict across generations, involving pain, suffering and mental anguish.

So what went wrong? We need to redefine the question we ask kids. When a child says that he wants to be a rock star, perhaps he means that he wants to as *famous* as his role model. He is attracted to the glamour and lifestyle of the artist but does not have the same passion for rock music. We need to ask what part about the rock star attracts him.

Instead of asking: 'What you want to *be*?' ask: 'What do you want to *do*?' What's the difference? After all, an engineer builds, a singer sings and a painter paints. The answer is: Huge. To dream of becoming a singer is fine, but when the child dreams of becoming a *famous* singer, that is troublesome. To become a singer the child can practice 18 hours a day and perfect his craft. But fame depends on many external factors not under his control. The weak links to fame can snap at anytime. Political events such as wars, social unrest, riots, cultural bindings and many other factors can become determining factors on the road to stardom. There are many artists who were *pulled* into stardom simply because of their lineage or because they had powerful mentors. Sometimes real talent gets overridden by average artists. Did their talent fail them? No. Could they have succeeded by working harder? I doubt it. Can they do something about it? I wonder. Will that leave the talented and overlooked ones bitter and lamenting for life? You bet! But if an actor or singer derives pleasure from indulging his craft, bitterness is not a corollary. Certainly he will feel bad about being overlooked, but he won't be broken. He will continue to sing or act.

Vincent Van Gogh, one of the post-impressionist masters, only managed to sell ONE painting in his entire life, that too, for just 400 francs. It left him bitter but did not lessen his joy in painting. He produced over 2,100 artworks, worth millions today. He loved to paint; that's what he did it. Posthumous recognition is not a fulfilling way of achieving success but sometimes that is how cruel life is. The best case is that we overcome our bitterness and continue enjoying what we like to do. The worst case is when bitterness ends only when life does.

There is a beautiful *shloka* in the *Bhagwad Gita* that says: 'Do your *karma* and do not worry about the result'. This simply means that you should do what is expected of you without attaching your actions to a success meter. If you are a singer, feel blessed. Work hard and concentrate on your art and excel in it. Do whatever is in your control, honestly and sincerely. If you have created a mental image of yourself as a famous star, it will hamper your performance. And here lies the crux. The weak link between you and stardom may just break and you may stop being famous. If that happens, it hurts deeply.

The *shloka* is part of the discourse that took place on a battlefield between Arjuna, a great warrior, and his mentor, Lord Krishna. Arjuna was confused about killing members of his own clan, for whom he had deep respect. Would he then be guilty of murder? And what good was a victory founded on the death of his elders? And the war would claim many on his side too. The great warrior lost his nerve. Abandoning his arms, Arjuna sat down dejected in his chariot. Krishna then motivated him to rise and fight saying words to the effect: 'You are supposed to be a warrior. All that should matter to you is that the war is just and that you have to fight. Don't lose yourself thinking of scenarios. You can win or you can lose. You can survive or die. Scenarios do not matter. They can be lived when the moment comes.' Though Lord Krishna's words were spoken to motivate Arjuna, they have proved to be an all-purpose guiding source of wisdom for Indian society and beyond.

Now let us return to the singer and what he should do. He should get his act together and practice hard, and have fun doing it. He should stop thinking of success or failure, being famous or flopping. That is not in his control. He can live it when the moment comes. Someone who writes because he loves writing, should continue to derive pleasure from it and not cloud his mind about missing the Booker. If he designs his work with an eye on the prize, two scenarios are possible – either the Booker will follow or he will be devastated. He may even quit writing. Similarly, scientists should do what they do for the joy of discovery, not tailor their research to win the Nobel.

MANAGING FAILURE

- Talk about your failures.
- Share your experiences.
- Learn from the failure of others.
- Like lightening, failure often strikes those who dare to fly high. But without the ability to take risks, there is no gain.
- Most failures happen because we are not paying attention to what is happening in our world. Pay attention and avoid stupid failures.
- Accept failure do happen. Do not live in denial. It is only when we accept it that anything meaningful can be done.
- Lend approval and support.
- Appreciate and celebrate the effort, whatever the result.
- Encourage and promote a risk-taking attitude. We can always use a safety net.
- Show respect for trying, not contempt for failing.

3. EMOTIONAL INTELLIGENCE: THE LANGUAGE AND POWER OF EMOTIONS

All learning has an emotional base. ~Plato

It is a well understood fact that what we excel in, we enjoy doing. When we do things we want to do, it does not feel like work and becomes a pleasure. If the learning process is designed in an interesting way, not only do we learn more, we look forward to it. Unfortunately, we have seen a shift whereby learning is forced upon children. What they learn and how they learn is determined by people more interested in achieving mass literacy than in building individual personalities.

The state of our emotions determines our success and happiness both at school and beyond. Positive emotions help us learn well while enabling better performance as we move forward in our lives. Some of us are naturally endowed with emotionally balanced minds and this reflects in our response to different situations. But not everyone is fortunate enough to take advantage of the emotional side of his mind. Such people lose out on the beneficial support of their emotional functions or suffer because of an inappropriate environment. Success or failure is influenced by how we respond and our responses stem from the state of our emotions.

The significance of emotions in our personal and professional lives has evolved as Emotional Intelligence (EI). Daniel Goleman, a psychologist, coined the term, describing ET as the ability to perceive, control and evaluate emotions. If we explore further, Emotional Intelligence an individual's ability to deal with his own emotions and relate to the emotions of others - empathy. It means how well we perceive and understand emotions and how we harness that power. Although called Emotional Quotient (once again bringing in the incorrigible human need to measure everything), 'intelligence' is an expression which better captures the essence of this unique human ability.

An emotionally intelligent person, for instance, understands anger and knows he is likely to take irrational decisions in a state of rage. He can thus prepare himself to act with restraint, knowing he may well repent his actions later. Most people behave irrationally under the influence of alcohol. An emotionally intelligent person identifies his limits and restricts his consumption. He is also aware of the effects of rage/alcohol on his friends, and is therefore able to play a restraining role which benefits all concerned.

At the board meeting of a courier company, while discussing expansion plans, the MD asked, 'How many centres do we have?'

The Operations Head replied, 'Sir, 1100'. The MD was infuriated. 'You have been here six months and are not even aware of the right number? Allow me to update your knowledge – we are 3000 strong.' The Operations Head, who knew the territory like the back of her hand, was stunned. She knew she was right but remained silent, unable to voice her dissent against the chief. Noticing her discomfort, her line boss quietly said, 'Sir, what she says is correct. There are 1100 centres while the rest are simply pick-up points.' The mood became obviously soured.

Let us analyze the situation. Both the MD and the Op Head were right in their own ways. But while the Op Head gave a factual answer, the MD wanted a holistic count. How can we know what the other person wants? Emotional Intelligence. The Op Head's line boss knew exactly what the MD wanted to *hear* from his team. The MD already *knew* the answer but wanted to hear it from his team. Emotional Intelligence helps us to bring to the fore what is expected and condition our minds accordingly.

EMOTIONAL INTELLIGENCE AND FAILURE

An emotionally intelligent person recognizes his fears and his susceptibility to failure. He conditions his mind to manage failure when it occurs, making the best of the situation. He channelizes the energy created by unfavourable events to learn, rather than plunging into hopelessness and depression. Emotional Intelligence enables him to rise above failure.

Emotional Intelligence is not being sentimental. It is important to understand the distinction. Being sentimental is getting affected by emotions and flowing along, making us liable to irrational actions. EI is about the *perception* of emotions, feeling but not flowing, or if flowing, it is a conscious decision.

Oscar Wilde said: A *sentimentalist is one who desires to have the luxury of an emotion without paying for it*. But having Emotional Intelligence is not only desirable, but an asset. An emotionally intelligent person is likely to keep his calm in stressful conditions and understand the emotional needs of those around them. EI is most essential in times of distress, for it is at such moments that both children and adults take undesirable actions.

Those who take the extreme step of ending their lives when facing failure, loss or rejection, are deficient in Emotional Intelligence. On the same measure, people who do not understand the pain and suffering of others are also EI deficient. A person with high EI accepts failure as a motivator, seeks the reasons for his failure, and works harder to overcome his shortcomings. At the same time, he empathizes with those suffering the pain of failure, just as he has.

DEVELOPING EMOTIONAL INTELLIGENCE

Can ET be developed? Earlier it was believed that like logical intelligence, a person was born with his share of Emotional Intelligence. While genetics play an important part, with appropriate exposure and training, Emotional Intelligence can be developed and enhanced. Laying greater stress on social values and work ethics, for instance, contributes towards this. Even simple acts like laughing at our mistakes, increases humility while making us more receptive towards other people's failures.

Emotional Intelligence needs to be recognized as an important characteristic in personality development rather than a soft skill and should be developed from early life. It helps not only in learning and growth but also in managing unfavourable situations. Buddha was once asked by a devotee, 'What have you gained from meditation?' He replied: 'Nothing. But what I lost was Anger, Anxiety, Depression, Insecurity, Fear of Old Age and Death.' The Buddha is perhaps the finest example of the one who motivated himself to develop his Emotional Intelligence. As we lose our negative emotions we strengthen our positive emotions.

4. ASK AND IT SHALL BE GIVEN. DO NOT ASK AND YOU WILL NOT RECIEVE.

A boy was having difficulty in lifting a heavy stone. As he was struggling, his father came by. Noting the boy's failure to move the stone despite his struggles, he asked, 'Are you using all your strength?''Yes, I am,' the boy replied. 'Well, I don't think you are,' the father said. 'I am right here, just waiting, and you haven't asked me to help you.'

This simple story, attributed to many different people, may not even be a true incident. But it captures in all its wonderful simplicity what massive tomes cannot. It reminds us of an important resource that we often fail to acknowledge or use. Many failures happen because we refuse to seek help. Sometimes all we have to do to succeed is ask for help. We know we need help. We know exactly what kind of help. We even know who can fulfil the requirement. Still, we do not ask. What follows is failure.

Why is it so difficult to ask for help? Why do we risk failure rather than ask? Here are some answers:

Fear of Rejection: We believe the request will be denied. Fear of rejection is a powerful deterrent. A denied request is often more damaging than failure to perform. Why do we assume our request will be rejected?

Fear of Obligation: We believe we will need to payback the favour. Seeking help become a matter of prestige, as well as a trade.

Symbol of Weakness: Seeking help is seen as accepting you are incapable of doing it on your own.

Sign of Failure: People don't want to be *seen* to be failing even when they are.

Cultural issues: Whether we seek the help of others is, to a great extent, influenced by culture. In collective cultures (such as in Asia), it is easier. The system is designed for interdependence to survive. But in individualistic cultures (such as America), it is difficult, as seeking help signifies weakness in an individual.

Our heroes and role models are important pointers about how we perceive seeking help. They are usually seen as highly individualistic people who help others, but rarely seek help themselves. Asking for help is a weakness heroes cannot afford. Asking for help is to identify your limitations. But the wise man knows that some things can only be done as a team.

Moral of the story: *It is smart to ask for help.* There is no point struggling and failing just to protect an image. Ask and accept. Get on with life.

5. WHY MOST PEOPLE FAIL IN THE RACE TO THE TOP

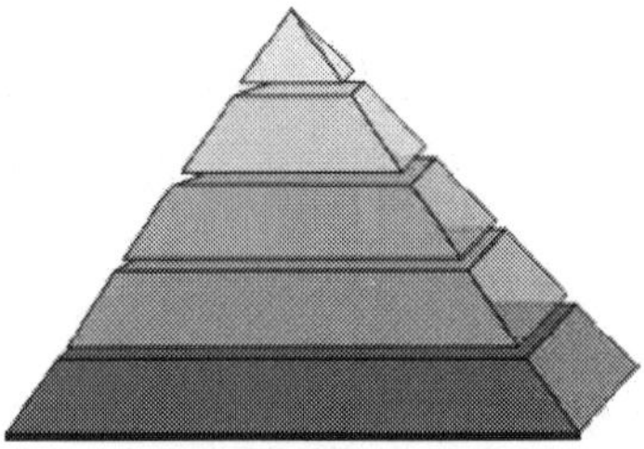

Everyone is running for the top, the corner office. Why? The biggest motivator is to climb the feudal pyramid which exists in every organization. Very few, however, reach there. Most fail and fall at various levels.

Why do most people fail? Are they not worthy of the top post? Ask those who decide and they will inevitably say they chose the best person for the job. Ask those who did not get the job and they will say there was foul play. One reason why the race to the top is always tough is because the entrance is narrow, only one spot.

Why do so many companies have hierarchical structures? Primarily because most of them started off as one-man shows and then expanded. That's the way most start-ups function. We hear so many stories of companies with humble beginnings, which grew to enter the Fortune 500 club. With each expansion, the control changed, like a king passing on the baton to his heir. The important fact was there was only one throne. So even if a number of equally competent persons competed for the top office, only one can be accommodated as CEO. That is the limitation of the system and has nothing to do with the competence of the individuals. The people do not fail; it is the system that fails the individuals.

The system works well where the company begins as an owner driven establishment and grows into a conglomerate. Since most companies begin this way, it has become the *de facto* norm. Everyone knows who the leader is (and held maximum stock), and who the heir was. It was a matter of control rather than prestige.

Then came companies that began as a democracy. They began with a group of close friends striking on an idea and taking collective decisions. But since the laws demanded a hierarchy, they elected one from among themselves to occupy the high chair and be their leader. They took turns at the top post.

Can there be a better organizational structure? The cube offers a more democratic distribution of power, with multiple tops and parallel carrier paths. Considering there is no single top, it certainly helps in easing pressure and eliminating a race to the top. A pyramid hierarchy merges control to a single top, the cubical organization with different control centres, offers a stable structure.

6. WHY PEOPLE AT THE TOP FAIL

Past performance does not guarantee future results, reads the standard disclosure by financial investment companies. The fact, however, is that we still believe that companies that have performed well in the past will continue to deliver in the future. Past performance is the basis of our trust. Why is it then that companies cannot guarantee their success? Is it a matter of risk or some other factor?

The Peter Principle is a management concept which avers that managers rise to the level of their incompetence. It means that a person who performs well is often rewarded with a higher position and responsibility. Eventually, he comes to hold a position beyond his competence level. This process is repeated till every position in the organization is occupied by people incompetent to carry out their assigned duties.

The reason for a person's incompetence may be the requirement of a different skill set. A person may be an excellent worker but lack interpersonal skills to manage and lead a team. The interesting thing is that the system prompts us to covet the position for which we are incompetent. We want promotion to a higher level even though we may not be suitable, because it is a symbol of prestige and progress. We simply cannot let it pass. Rather we go to any lengths to attain it.

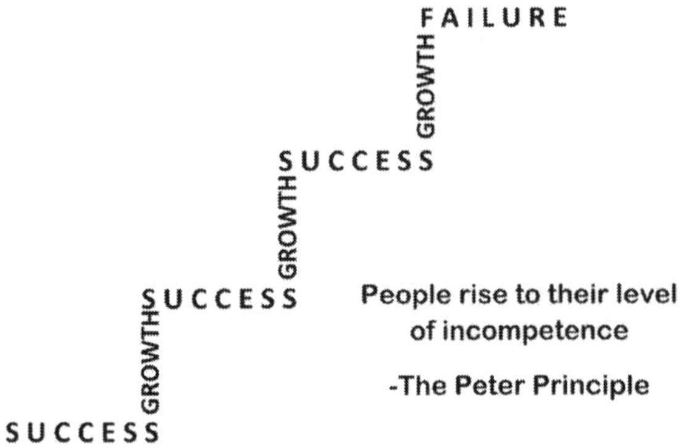

7. WHY LEADERS FAIL

Dunning and Kruger proposed the idea that people cannot judge their true abilities and knowledge. Those who have a command over a subject feel there is still much to know. They are humble enough to recognize their limitations. But those with superficial knowledge, believe they have mastered the subject. The truly knowledgeable live in self-doubt; the ones with shallow knowledge come to occupy the top positions, purely on their self-confidence.

'If you're incompetent, you can't know you're incompetent. And the skills you need to produce a right answer are exactly the skills you need to recognize what a right answer is,' said David Dunning in an interview to NY Times. The theory can be used to derive some deeper facts. Dunning and Kruger proposed that incompetent people:

- fail to recognize their own lack of skill;
- fail to recognize genuine skill in others;
- fail to recognize the extent of their inadequacy.

The Peter Principle and Dunning-Kruger Effect can perhaps be combined to produce the Unified Theory of Failure in Organizations. The Peter Principle tells us how and why incompetent people rise to decision-making positions, while the Dunning-Kruger Effect tells us what happens when they actually occupy the high chair. The Unified Theory of Failure declares that the incompetent rise to the top and once there, fail to recognize the skills/qualities of genuine people and promote the unworthy to positions of significance. By claiming superiority, they reject all feedback. The truly knowledgeable ones meanwhile, develop lower profiles, underestimating their own potential, assuming that if they can do a particular job, anyone can. Holding lower rung positions, they are rarely empowered to bring about positive change.

8. WHY WE FAIL TO NOTICE AND ADAPT TO CHANGE

There are two aspects to the above statement:

1. We fail to notice change.
2. We fail to adapt to the change happening around us.

The first statement is perhaps not entirely correct because it is not that we do not notice change, but we avoid, ignore and resist it.

Failure and change share a strong relationship. Like failure, change too, is inevitable. Perhaps, when we think of change, the thought of failure pulls us back. It is not change itself that scares us but the fear of failure. It clouds the mind, forcing us to avoid, ignore and resist change. According to research, about 70% of all change initiatives fail (i.e. 70% of time people look the other way or defend their positions rather than accept change).

Why do social changes fail? Traditions strive to maintain the past; change breaks the status quo. Traditions are resistant to change, primarily because they provide us with a road map we have become accustomed to over time. Even the pitfalls of that road are acceptable to us, for over the years we have developed ways to work around them. We fear that straying from our known road can bring trouble. Adapting to a new path would mean re-formulating work-around mechanisms for new points of failure.

Change also means that the mechanisms we have developed over time are no longer effective, while the newer ways might just fail. Thus, change brings the fear of letting go of established norms, replacing them with uncertainty. These twin factors cause our paranoia about change. The best change is gradual, blending with prevailing traditions.

Why does change happen? Most changes begin with the question: *Why*? At some point someone becomes dissatisfied and raises the question of why it is so. Then he engages his mind to discover the reasons. Dissatisfaction is thus the key driver of all change. Most people, however, are comfortable with the prevailing system and view change as a threat. Therefore, we resist.

INDIVIDUALISM VS COLLECTIVISM

We all know it is easier for an individual to change than for a whole group or community to adapt as individuals adapt at their own pace. How does this observation help our understanding of why change fails?

Cultures founded on collectivism, like Asian societies, resist change. It is far more difficult to introduce change into traditional societies. Change is first resisted, or if accepted, it is slow to spread. But once it is accepted, it stays in place for a long time. This is also the reason why Asian immigrants are slow to adapt to Western ways. But traditional societies exhibit a unique characteristic: resilience. Traditional societies focus on survival and stability; they wait for change to happen and settle, and *then* adapt.

In individualistic societies, change is easier to accept and more likely to succeed. New ideas and inventions are easier to develop and adapt to, but switches happen just as quickly when the next changeover arrives. Individualistic societies focus on survival by quickly adapting to change. They show little resilience.

What we call failure to change may, when seen from another perspective, be a matter of resilience.

9. THE CO-RELATION BETWEEN SUCCESS AND TRAVELLING

Trees are interesting. They are born in a spot of earth from a tiny seed and grow into structures of fabulous dimensions. They spend their lives in the same place. In their life-cycle, standing in one place, trees see many seasons. Every cycle they survive is marked by a ring in their trunks. Most of us are like trees. We spend our whole lives in the place we know, rarely moving away. Like trees, we remain rooted, growing up and growing old as we watch the seasons of our lives pass by.

But in times of adversity, such as prolonged drought, trees die. They don't move to where there is water and nutrition. They cannot. But people can. Yet most of us remain rooted, restraining ourselves, denying ourselves our true potential. We do not seek new opportunities. In the history of humankind, wealth has been created by two kinds of people – traders and conquerors. Both involved travelling. Migrants travel to where opportunity lies.

In earlier times, humans moved whenever resources became insufficient to sustain life. In modern times, people move across continents in search of opportunities to grow. Are those who are prepared to venture forth, accepting the dangers of being uprooted from the familiar, more successful than native dwellers? Apparently, yes. Migrants are successful because they are willing to follow the sun of opportunity. Native dwellers, on the other hand, are constrained by familial and neighbourhood ties; they seek educational and employment opportunities in a localized area. Given the same opportunities, political stability and social security, those who do not limit themselves are more likely to succeed. Migrants do better because they *choose* their place of migration and do not hesitate to move again if things become difficult.

So why do we limit ourselves? What stops us from travelling and seeking new opportunities? The most important factor is culture and the society we live in. Even recently, traditional-minded Indians feared crossing the seas, which were considered both sacred and dangerous. Crossing the waters involved loss of caste.

If we are not ready to move, for whatever reasons, we may be seriously lowering our chances of success. However, we may still attain emotional and psychological happiness.

10. FAILURE MANAGEMENT TIPS FROM BOXING

Does getting punched hurt? Yes. Can you ensure not being hit? No. In the ring, no one can guarantee a punch-free bout. And you never know when a David will defeat a Goliath by landing blows at strategic points. In the course of the fight we can get hurt, but then we do have a choice here. We can simply opt out, or we can train ourselves to survive. Mistakes and failures happen. But if we want to be part of the game, we have to prepare to deal with the blows that failure delivers. Delivering knockout punches comes with training but surviving such blows requires conditioning.

How do we train? It is difficult to escape getting hit, so start with learning to diffuse the blows. A boxer is trained to move his body with the punch. This technique is popularly called 'rolling with the hit'. What seems a jaw-crusher, is actually a trained response to take such a blow. The boxer is trained to lessen the impact of the punch by moving in the same direction. Though it may seem less heroic, rolling with the punch diffuses the impact.

Another training technique is to always keep the eyes open. We have to see what is coming at us. It is a common reflex to close both eyes when a blow lands. But then one misses the other fist coming in. The second blow has the power to knock us out. The punch-line: A failure has occurred with the first blow; do not close your eyes to the bigger danger hurtling your way.

An interesting statistic exists about victims of vehicle hits. Usually, the impact of the collision knocks the person out. But the real damage is caused by the other vehicles on the road, often crushing the victim as he lies immobile. Usually, just before getting hit, the victim becomes aware of the danger and even tries to avoid it. But it is the second danger, which he cannot see, that causes the most severe damage. It is the second hit that usually proves to be the knock-out punch.

II. AUTOBIOGRAPHIES AND BIOGRAPHIES

Does reading autobiographies and biographies serve any purpose? After all, they are about other people's lives, lived in different times. The circumstances were not similar to ours. What happened and how they reacted cannot concern us. Many great men and women were not well read persons. In fact, some had only basic education while others were even illiterate. By reading *My Experiments With Truth*, I cannot become a Gandhi. His times were different, as were the issues he fought for. His reactions were different from ours today. Steve Jobs, the IT icon, famously said: *Your time is limited, so don't waste it living someone else's life.*

Most successful people don't really know how they got there. The fact is that every success story has a different 'how'. There is no pattern. But for people who failed, it is different. They know why or what undid their efforts. These are the people one needs to seek out and learn from them the pitfalls in the path to success. People who have failed can be good teachers. People who have failed and then succeeded (learning from their failures), are excellent teachers. If you know such people, kneel at their feet and beg them to become your guru.

The best read biography in India is the *Ramayana*, describing the life and times of Lord Rama. Why is it considered the greatest story ever told? Because we learn from both success and failure – the success of Lord Rama and the failure of Ravana, Lord of Lanka. One of the most inspiring passages comes at the end, as Ravana, the symbol of arrogance, lies wounded, waiting for the end. Lord Rama tells his brother, Lakshmana, to seek advice from the dying king. A bewildered Lakshmana asks, 'What advice can a king who is defeated possibly give? We have won and we are the ones who should be giving advice to the people on statecraft and fighting wars.' Rama replies: *The man who lies there dying is a master of all knowledge. He lies there, fallen, because of his mistakes. Learn from his follies so that you don't repeat them.* The words of the dying king, recounting his failures to the victor prince, remain guidelines for Indian society.

Successes often happen accidently – the classic case being the apple falling on Newton's head, resulting in the discovery of the law of gravity. Another often quoted example is Michael Faraday's discovery of electromagnetic induction (EMI), which revolutionised Physics. Faraday was working on a problem for a long time but was unable to get results. In his frustration he threw a magnet he was holding across the room. The magnet, by a quirk of fate, passed through a magnetic coil and caused the needle of the galvanometer attached to the coil to move. Now, the needle moves only when current flows through it. The thrown magnet moving through the coil had induced current to flow. Faraday saw the needle move. It led to the theory of magnetic induction.

Let us analyse these historical incidents. Was the discovery of gravity really an accidental discovery? Was it the first time Newton had seen an apple (or anything else) falling? Considering that he was in his mid-forties, he must have seen many things fall. But none of them triggered a brainwave. Why? He was working on critical issues for which he could find no solution. He was experiencing *failure*. His mind was extra perceptive. Had it not been the falling apple, Newton would have noticed something else. Now, let us re-read the EMI story. Faraday too, was unable to get results. He was *failing* and frustrated. When does frustration set in? When you try repeatedly and yet failure stares you in the face.

Biographies are not just interesting incidents put together. If we read carefully, there is a wealth of experience to learn from. What the above stories tell us it that these two failing scientists were not banging their heads or lamenting their failure. In fact, they were razor sharp and ready when opportunity presented itself. Repeated failures did not prevent them from keeping their minds open. Why? Because they enjoyed what they did and continued doing it. They were there for the love of science, which spells of failure could not touch.

There are many instances of people becoming successful accidentally. Bollywood has numerous examples of roles being given to someone because the original choice for the part was either unavailable or uninterested. That *someone* became an overnight success and the movie went on to become an all-time hit. Some of those *someones'* became stars, overshadowing the actors who once rejected the original roles.

Amitabh Bachchan is perhaps the most successful superstar in Hindi cinema but he had done many movies which failed to make a mark. In 1973, Director Prakash Mehra was casting for his movie *Zanjeer and* wanted to cast Raj Kumar in the lead. Raj Kumar refused. The role was then offered to three more stars - Dharmendra (who was busy elsewhere), Dev Anand (who wanted to sing as well), and Rajesh Khanna, the first superstar of Hindi cinema (who saw it as a spoiler for his image as romantic hero). Amitabh Bachchan was the fifth choice for the film that established him as the angry young man, the social rebel, an image which dominated the scene for the next two decades. Within five years, the other four had quietly passed into oblivion.

Bollywood is full of such accidental successes and failures. The question is: Of the five movie stars, did the legendary four who made the famous rejections, actually *fail?* Was this an accidental success or accidental failures? Most accidental stars who land dream roles are either struggling or have failed to make an impact with their earlier work. But (and this is important), they did not quit. They wanted to work and made themselves available; they lobbied hard. What mattered was that they showed up and were ready to grab opportunity when it came. Woody Allen once said that 80% of success is showing up.

The success we achieve depends on our hard work and willingness to perform (show up). Of course, what constitutes the other 20% of the equation is very interesting; the 80% activity only works if the 20% does.

12. AUTHORS: TOPPING THE FAILURE CHARTS

Authors top the failure list. More than being read, they dream of being written about. Is that not strange? Actually, it is not. Most of authors have a top-top approach – they believe in beginning their careers from a peak of fame and remaining there for the rest of their lives. They live with the notion that anything coming from their pen (or laptop), is profound and the world must applaud their masterpiece. And that is precisely why they fail. Authors write; readers read and judge.

Why do authors write? The technical answer is they have something to communicate – stories, anecdotes, views or even an account of their own lives. Why do they want to tell stories? They think they are good at it? They want to make a living telling stories? Acclaim? Perhaps the fear of oblivion keeps them ticking?

The most entertaining stories are the ones authors tell themselves. But halfway through their work, writers begin building an aura and living celebrity lives. They approach publishers with the demand their work be published. It is only when the publisher holds up a mirror that a reality check occurs. Then it hurts. And that is when authors become frustrated writers.

Publishers run for-profit businesses. They make choices as shopkeepers do – keeping only those products that will sell. If the product will not sell, they don't want it. Of course, the larger shops have the ability to push products through clever placements but you can go only so far with that. Repeat orders only come when customers like the product. Just as store owners employ people to help him choose and push the right product, publishers hire people to help him choose the right product.

What *is* the right product? The one that sells. These creative people are burdened with the duty of selecting possible winners. They manage the store and decide which products are in demand, what people will like and what will come back to be pulped. How do they decide? They study tastes and trends, the current flavours in demand. And what if people want a change and decide to try a different flavour? The store is stuck with some unsellable products.

But there is another angle to the story. When selectors chose the right products, they also *reject* those which (according to them), are not saleable. That is why books like *The Fountainhead once* garnered comments like, 'Unsaleable and unpublishable'. A quick Google search of initially rejected bestsellers will give you a fair idea of how often the decision-makers were wrong. So were the products rejected initially because they were bad products? Some were, certainly. But there is a fair chance they were rejected because the managers opined that people would not like them.

So who succeeded and who failed? The author happened to prepare a dish the managers thought unsavoury and did not serve. The author had thus to wait till tastes changed or set up his own shop. So did the managers fail in their judgment? We do not know how the editors who rejected JK Rowling and Agatha Christie reacted but this is what a senior editor at a large publishing house said in her article,

One Mistake of My Life after rejecting Chetan Bhagat's *Five Point Someone*; the book later caused a major shift in Indian publishing and Bhagat became a bestselling author with cult status:*...and to this day, our boss complains bitterly that he missed out on the biggest bestseller of the decade because he went by the judgment of three Bengali women – a flawed demographic, if there ever was one! The subsequent glossy product looks at me reproachfully (even sneeringly) from the shelves of bookshops, from the shoulders of 'traffic lights booksellers', at railway stations and airports. I guess I'll always share the dubious distinction of having turned down Indian publishing's biggest commercial success!*

While Chetan Bhagat showed nerves of steel and finally got his revenge by attaining stardom, not every author who faces rejection takes it in his stride. Those who take the call may have destroyed quite a few budding pens because they produced something very different from the norm. Or worse, they could have pushed the gifted and talented into the anonymous world of ghost-writing.

Moral of the story:

Authors:

- Concentrate on what you do; keep calm and write.
- Keep your feet on the ground. You can save yourself a fall.
- Do your research about popular flavours. Tailor your creation. Then you will be allowed to serve your broth.
- It is better to stick to your original recipe. Tastes change.
- Understand the compulsions of publishers. A rejection is not a death warrant. Neither is it *Vox Dei*, the voice of God.
- Review and revise. Show and discuss your work with friends. Seek feedback.

Publishers:

- Engage with the author. The least you can do is communicate with the poor guy and say something. A few lines of feedback can save someone anxious moments and perhaps deliver a Booker.

13. RESILIENCE

We sometimes take extreme steps while reacting to failure. Microtrauma is the body's natural way of dealing with small injuries. Muscle-skin-tendon stress and tears occur in the course of our day-to-day activities. Interestingly, the body knows each time a tear or abrasion occurs, and tries to rebuild it. The repaired part is tougher and more resilient to injuries.

The Chinese were perhaps the first to understand and apply the science behind microtrauma to convert the body into a weapon. Chinese martial arts use the knowledge of microtrauma to cause repeated minor injuries to the body in order to build heavier, thicker and tougher muscle fibre which is more resistant. Similarly, they use techniques like punching into hot sand and wooden boards, using both palms and fingers. This causes skin damage. The body responds by building tougher skin, harder than before. The training continues till the body becomes tough. The fingers of a trained martial arts exponent can be as hard as steel, capable of causing severe damage. Using microtrauma, the Chinese inflict failure in order to compel the body to become better.

Microtrauma is also used to build muscle in the gym. Every time you lift an extra load or push weights, the body muscles experience trauma. Soon, the body builds tougher and thicker muscles, tendons and fibres. Similarly, a sailor's palms develop thicker and tougher skin, capable of handling more stress.

The mind too, works on the same principle. The more we exert and push it, the better it gets. And the more we *avoid* doing something, the poorer our performance becomes. The more we fear, the more painful it becomes.

The Thesis: We can develop resilience by introducing micro-failures. Dealing with micro-failures strengthens us mentally and protects us from the effects of major failure shock. We are better being prepared as failure can push a person into deep depression.

14. THE SIGNIFICANCE (OR INSIGNIFICANCE) OF AWARDS

If Award = Success, does No Award = Failure?

If Best = Success, does Second-Best = Failure?

What do awards mean? Do awards do more harm than good? Is there a case for abolishing all awards? For every award given, there are many who are left out. For every success, there are many who are branded as failures and pass into oblivion. Instead of encouraging healthy competition, awards often stress failure. How often have you heard, 'the competition is killing me'? Competing for awards and records is not just killing us, but destroying us morally and psychologically.

Awards are believed to be a measure of success, but missing out on them should not mean failure. Historically, many scientists, authors and artists have been denied recognition. Awards are a continuation of our primitive past, distinguishing a few from the rest. The basic perception is that awards are granted to honour the best for exemplary service or achievement, when, in fact, they may stand for something completely different.

Kautilya, popularly known as Chanakya, was a master-administrator and mentor to Emperor Chandragupta Maurya. The duo were responsible for building the foundations of the great Mauryan empire, which at its peak covered most of the Indian sub-continent. Chanakya laid down elaborate procedures for maintaining order and harmony in the empire that lasted for over 200 years. The broad policy came to be known as *Chanakya Neeti*. The most popular policy is the five-point *Sam- Daam- Dand- Bhed–Upeksha Neeti*

- *Sam*, meaning *samman*, use of awards, honours and praise.
- *Daam*, meaning use of money – monetary help, donations, loans and gifts.
- *Dand*, meaning fear of authority – punishment, waging war, crushing rebellions.
- *Bhed* has multiple meanings and each is an important aspect of the policy:

- to breach – implying divide and rule;
- differences – creating/using the differences among your opponents to your advantage;
- discrimination – using this art to your advantage;
- mystery – not everything a ruler does should be obvious to the people; some things need to shrouded in mystery;
- secrets – knowing the secrets of your opponents can prove decisive. The Mauryans had a strong spy network, which spread across the empire.

➢ *Upeksha,* meaning to ignore. Ignoring someone can be a powerful force in making him perform.

Chanakya used the primitive art of honouring to create a special class in society. Honouring promoted loyalty as the welfare of the honoured became attached to the ruler's. Therefore the policy was more to promote the interests of the ruling class than to bring out the best among the masses. Most nations and corporates around the world use the *Chanakya Neeti* in some form to maintain order.

Another important aspect of awards was to keep the people competing among themselves. This kept them engaged and dissipated their energies. Denied this outlet, the people could have directed their energies against the state itself. Next time your name is up for the *Best Employee Award*, visualize your colleagues competing and plotting to bring you down. If some of them become your arch rivals, you will know it is the management playing games with all of you as pawns.

The Nobel Prize is the most prestigious of awards and every many names, all worthy and renowned in their respective fields, are recommended for the award. And every year the list of those who missed the Nobel Prize keeps growing. The awardees naturally become celebrities while those who missed out (each as illustrious as the awardees), continue their lives, vying for university medals. How does the world view those who missed out? As failures?

Up to 1960, the Nobel Peace Prize was awarded almost exclusively to Europeans and Americans. Over the years, the Nobel committee has had a tough time explaining their choices and rejections. 'I was very happy to know that the Nobel Prize was not awarded to me,' said Leo Tolstoy, when asked how he felt on being left out. 'It deprived me of a big problem of how to use this money. I am certain that this money...can only bring evil.'

Gandhi was nominated in 1937, 1938, 1939, 1947, and finally a few days before he was murdered in January 1948. The failure to award him the Nobel has been publicly regretted by later members of the Nobel committee. When the Dalai Lama was awarded the Peace Prize in 1989, the chairman of the committee said it was 'in part a tribute to the memory of Mahatma Gandhi'. However, the committee has never commented on why Gandhi was not awarded the prize. While the whole world was celebrating Gandhi as a global peace icon, the Noble committee was unsure, five times.

Even though the list of those overlooked for the Nobel is extensive and beyond the scope of this book, the case of Mendeleev needs to be mentioned. The great chemist who gave us the fundamental tool to understand chemistry: the periodic table, was nominated twice, in 1905 and 1906, but one committee member thought his contributions were too old and well-known.

Did denial of the Nobel Prize make Leo Tolstoy and Mahatma Gandhi failures or Mendeleev less of a scientist? Did they introduce their contributions to society anyway? Awards are often given to surprising people, leaving us to wonder why so and so missed out. Does missing out on awards mean failure? Anyone who says, 'the objective of my life is to win a Nobel/Oscar/ Grammy/Booker one day, so let me prepare for it,' is a phony. We need to stop chasing awards as these have been reduced to commodities. We must remember that awards are decided by a group of persons who have their own ideologies and philosophies to promote. If anyone does not fall into their criteria, it does not mean his work has become meaningless.

Why are we discussing the hits and misses of the Nobel Prize? Because it is considered the most honourable of all awards and this makes people covet it. The basic concept of awards creates a race among professions and professionals, each racing to publish research papers first, even though others have arrived at the same conclusion independently. The findings of the person presenting first, are acclaimed, while the same findings by someone presenting later, are ignored. Thus, aware people rush to publish their basic idea in journals and win while the less aware individuals wait for the complete results of their research and in so doing, lose the award. Often institutions stand for or against particular individuals, making it a battle of prestige. Battle? We are discussing awards, right?

The writer who accepts an honour of this kind involves as well as himself the association or institution which has honoured him. The writer must therefore refuse to let himself be transformed into an institution, wrote Jean-Paul Sartre to the Swedish Academy when he refused the Nobel. He also refused to accept the Legion of Honour, the highest award in France.

The most common riposté is that awards create healthy competition, leading to development. Awards provide motivation to do something better.

AWARDS AT SCHOOL

We have all kinds of awards in school to motivate the young. Actually, what schools do is encourage students to compete among themselves, thereby creating divisions and classifying them into achievers, average performers and non-performers. Children are ranked and graded repeatedly as every effort is made to sort 'the best' from the rest.

But are not schools in the business of empowering children and enhancing creativity? Are we not discussing centres of learning here? It looks like a battle to win awards. Even at six years of age, children compete and seek to win at any cost, with their parents joining in. What values are we inculcating in our children? Competition creates a rift between students: My group vs your group; my class vs your class. It becomes I/We against You/Yours. It is never about Us. Ironically, we preach togetherness.

Failing to get an award often has devastating effects on people. Creative professions such as authors, singers, actors, and artists, are more sensitive to the hurt and can plunge into depression. To a twelve-year-old, the 'Best of Class' award is no less coveted. Failing to get it can severely impact his psyche. Awards are believed to motivate students, but for every motivated student there are 40 odd devastated ones who feel deprived and dejected. In another light, they are perhaps being hardened for real life, where there will experience bias, strings being pulled, and winning by any means, fair or foul.

Awards and rewards are motivating for a few, for a limited time. Once the student is mature enough to assess the best and worst case scenarios (the maximum he will gain (reward) and the maximum he will lose (punishment)) he will require greater incentive to confirm. The stimulii to perform has to be increased at regular intervals.

Both reward and punishment are ways to manipulate behaviour, prompting the questions, 'What do they want me to do? And what do I get for doing it?' Neither reward nor punishment helps children grapple with, 'What kind of person do I want to be?' Alfie Kohn, in his article, 'The Risks of Rewards', suggests that the more we want children to *want* to do something, the more counter-productive it is to reward them for doing it.

The award and reward system is crying out to be abolished. A more meaningful system needs to be devised, with the focus on learning together rather than on individual performance. Creating star students only makes the other students feel deprived.

15. THE STRANGE CASE OF GHOST WRITERSAND ARTISTS

Why do people write? From a desire to seem clever; to be talked about; to be remembered; to get their own back on those who snubbed them in childhood? George Orwell wrote that one of the motivations to write was sheer egoism.But even egoism dissolves in the face of the need to survive. So writers often become ghosts - nameless and faceless - living behind another person's persona.

Years ago, I got hooked to the Hardy Boys. I searched the local libraries for every edition and wanted to know the smallest detail about their creator. Strangely, I could not find anything about Franklin W. Dixon. The paperbacks carried no picture of the author so I began looking at hard bound editions in elite bookstores. Many years later, I came to know that the greatest mystery of the Hardy Boys, was that F.W. Dixon, their creator, was as fictitious as Frank and Joe Hardy, the heroes of the series. FWD did not exist. The series was created by publisher, Edward Stratemeyer. He hired writers to write under the pen name F.W. Dixon. The pseudonym was the property of Stratemeyer Syndicate, a book-packaging company.

What is a book-packaging company? One that puts together books using a team of writers, editors, proof readers, designers and printers. They then sell the books to publishers. Stratemeyer Syndicate hired different authors to write as FWD, starting with Leslie McFarlane, a Canadian journalist, who answered an ad placed by the company. The same syndicate was responsible for producing Nancy Drew, where numerous authors were employed to write under the name Carolyn Keene.

It was most disappointing to learn the truth. Over the years I had created a mental image of the unknown author putting together the characters in the Hardy Boys series. Reading creates a bond between author and reader. We assume that when authors write, they are recounting/using incidences from their own life experiences. To discover that books were manufactured, like other products, in a book factory, by faceless, nameless people, somehow damaged my respect for the books themselves. Nothing changed materially; the stories were the same, as was the narration, but the aura was gone.

We do not know who crated up the soap we use or the cola we drink. Nor do we care, as long as the soap and cola continue to give us satisfaction. Stratemeyer created a brand (quite a few actually). Not by chance but by design – placing ads for writers. He planned to set up a book producing factory because that was his trade. He did it at a grand level and created some very successful brands. He was the Henry Ford of book publishing. Like Henry Ford, who pioneered the assembly line for automobiles, Stratemeyer put together the assembly line for producing books, employing many staff who performed specific functions. Even today, new Hardy Boys stories are being published. The product has become a brand like Coca Cola.

The realization that there was no FW Dixon shattered the mental image I had built. Today, my once prized and cherished collection, put together so painstakingly, has lost its sheen, reduced to the level of pulp fiction. Perhaps it is I who have aged and am no longer excited by the adventures of the adolescent brothers, but that is not the entire story. There is a sense of been cheated – like discovering that the most adventurous and heroic scenes in a movie were done by an unknown double.

Not that the writers engaged were not talented. They did, after all create heroes from their imagination, entertaining us, and continuing to do so. Were they failures? Had the writers been able to publish works under their own name, the world would have placed them in the hall of fame. Unfortunately, they did not have the resources to do so and became dependant on book producers. Some of them did try to establish their identity but succumbed to the tide of rejections from publishers.

The tribe of ghost writers has always existed, evolving and surviving in different avatars. They appear as speechwriters for politicians, manuscript writers for celebrities (most autobiographies are ghost written), and vanity publishing (people who wish to be projected as authors to gain prestige). Perhaps the most important works in the history of mankind were ghost-written. The same is true of most religious texts, where different scholars combined their work to produce the final product. Collective wisdom never becomes dissociated from such works.

We have no qualms about hiring a cook or a driver, so why is hiring a writer to write for us seem so unethical? Is it because it is an act of impersonation? Traditionally writing has always been considered a noble endeavour. The written word has always held authority. It is difficult to argue against the written word. If you want to prove anything, it has to be written down. Today we may have Wikipedia to believe in and Google to lead us, but in earlier times, the scriptures as the written word, was believed to be divine.

Without the written tablet citing the Ten Commandments, it Moses could not have convinced his people. The written tablet was proof of God's word. Indians associate Goddess Saraswati with the written word and wisdom. The underlying belief is that to create something brings the author closer to god. To be an author is therefore an act of faith. Hence, when we realize someone else was responsible for the writings, that faith is broken. What if the Ten Commandments had been ghost-written? Would we believe in them as the word of God?

If foolproof evidence is presented that William Shakespeare employed a number of writers and passed off their work as his, would we think differently of him? Would we consider him a fake? But would the world stop reading and appreciating those plays? How about Da Vinci? Would the Mona Lisa lose her charm if it was discovered she was painted by some unknown assistant? Or that the Sistine Chapel ceiling was done by a number of artists working under Michelangelo?

Peter Paul Rubens, a much sought after painter of the renaissance, is known to have employed a battery of talented artists at his studio, each trained to paint in his style. He would provide the sketches and the assistants would work on them. Finally he would give the paintings the finishing touches. In his studio, 80 easels were set up. When a client came to visit, he would send all his assistants away and move along the rows of easels, painting feverishly. The client was left awed by his talent and energy.

Do you marvel at those nameless assistants? Do you shake your head over their potential or sympathize with them for being denied the fame that was rightfully theirs?

END WORD

In the summer of 1993, two friends, A and B, graduated from the same University. They both saw a newspaper advert about a reputed Open University launching a Master's programme in computer applications. The applicants were required to clear an entrance test. A and B both appeared for the exam. A was successful, B was not. A celebrated while B sat depressed. In fact, the Open University in question had a quota system in order to get students with varied academic backgrounds. So, while B's three years of electronics did not carry any weight, A with three years in life sciences did.

Dejected by his failure, B joined a company's computer department as a trainee. At a seminar he met a senior executive who told him about an opening in California. B flew to the US, where he spent five years. He returned to head the company's India operations.

What happened to A? The new course he joined was the first batch at the Open University and the infrastructure was not yet in place. The course material was still nebulous. The University had tied up with private computer education providers for practical training. These companies were more interested in billing the University by the hour than in providing services to the students. While B was getting real life experience in Mumbai and then in California, A was trying to get through the course. Finally A became frustrated and left, justifying his actions saying that even Bill Gates had dropped out. But A was no Bill Gates. He was neither adequately educated nor experienced. He was unemployable. He began an IT venture with a friend but could not first clients. He became dependent on his family.

So who failed and who succeeded? Was B lucky in failing to be selected for the Open University programme? It certainly looked like it. But A, who believed he had a secure future, woke up to a nightmare. Imagine both A and B sitting in a pub in different cities.

While A mourned how a success skewed his life path, B would be rejoicing that a failure forced him to chalk out an alternate path. Failure is as much a part of the game as success. We could all be A or B at some point of time, feeling elated or dejected, and then seeing a turnaround. There are no rules for handling failure, just as there is no grammar for success. Failure is painful but then, success too, can be difficult to handle.

There are so many stories about people have shown resilience and bounced back after facing failure. Similarly, there are many cases of people showing extraordinary talent in their earlier years but making little use of it in their adult lives. There also cases where success or failure just *happened*. People call it circumstance or luck (good or bad). Success is not a mathematical formula which, if executed perfectly, can assure you a certain win every time. You cannot have a situation where success is the only option. As JK Rowling put it: *It is impossible to live without failing at something, unless you live so cautiously that you might as well not have lived at all – in which case, you fail by default.*

The eternal question is: Are we successful because of our passion or does our passion grow from our success? Passion certainly helps but it is not always the determining factor. Just passion is not enough. In crossing a rickety bridge, one has to keep a cool head, *especially* when a rotten plank gives way. Worry yourself to death does not help. Do not lose your head when it is most required.

The best way to cross a shaky bridge is to know its weaknesses. Know the risks involved. Know that there are rotten planks that may give way. Devise a strategy and then, working a step at a time and testing each plank, make your moves. Passion may be the motivator, but the falling planks are the reality. A plank falling is a failure of plan but only part of the final crossing. It should be treated as such. Remember: Do not follow the falling plank; you need to cross the bridge.

Failure is not always a bad thing rather an exposure to failure has spurred the careers of some very famous people. How? They learned from their failures and became wiser. They took care not to repeat their mistakes. Imagine the rickety old bridge again. You are fired up with passion to cross over to the other end. Only it is still dark as you, fired up by your passion, could not wait for the day break. Consider these scenarios:

- As you step on the first plank, it breaks and you stumble, but you save yourself from falling.
- After clearing a few planks easily, your foot slips and suddenly you find yourself halfway down the bridge, flailing wildly to find support.

Which is the better option – early failure acting as a wake-up call or a sudden fall? Be thankful for early failures. They prevent a fall.

So should we promote failure? We need to teach people how to handle and learn from unfavourable results; how to find the silver lining and make the best of a situation. Allow children to observe how others cross the same rickety bridge. Then, with harness in place let them experience failures first hand. Sensitize children to failure in a positive way. Tell them it is okay to fail. Just as a child who gets hurt does not stop playing, someone who fails should not stop trying.

Insults and humiliation are advanced developments in a society where mental hurt causes more pain than physical torture. The idea behind social reprimand was to make a person realize his actions were not acceptable and needed to change. We have followed this path with limited success.

Instead, why not forgive others their failures? And why not forgive ourselves as well? There is no need to commit *hara-kiri*.

Give success another chance.

NOTES

Section I Failure Hurts
India is Suicide Capital: World Health Organisation (WHO)http://www.ndtv.com/article/india/india-is-suicide-capital-world-health-organisation-who-586771

Section II First Encounter
'No detention' policy workshttp://www.thehindu.com/news/cities/chennai/no-detention-policy-works/article3429830.ece
No-fail till Class 8 may be reviewed
http://www.hindustantimes.com/india-news/newdelhi/no-fail-till-class-8-may-be-reviewed/ar ticle1-1052440.aspx
'No-fail policy has only hurt children'
http://timesofindia.indiatimes.com/city/nagpur/No-fail-policy-has-only-hurt-children/articleshow/40831982.cms
No-detention till Class 8,students in for reality check in Class 9, **Vivek Gupta, Hindustan Times** Chandigarh, March 19, 2014
http://www.hindustantimes.com/punjab/chandigarh/no-detention-till-class-8-students-in-for-reality-check-in-class-9/article1-1196992.aspx

Section III The Failure Factor
http://www.businessinsider.in/When-I-Asked-Jeff-Bezos-The-Tough-Questions-No-Profits-The-Book-Controversies-The-Phone-Flop-He-Proved-Why-Hes-A-Genius-CEO/articleshow/45507079.cms
Section IV, The Anatomy of Failure
Bill Richardson, Sonny Nwankwo & Susan Richardson, *Understanding the Causes of Business Failure Crises: Generic Failure Types: Boiled Frogs, Drowned Frogs, Bullfrogs and Tadpoles* (Management Decision, Vol. 32: 4, 1994, pp. 9-22)

Section V The Psychology of Failure
Wings of Fire Dr APJ Abdul Kalam, Arun Tiwari Universities Press (1999)
My Journey: Transforming Dreams into Actions. Dr APJ Abdul Kalam, Rupa Publications India, 2013
The Race of My Life: Milkha Singh, Rupa Publications
The amazing Infosys story
http://specials.rediff.com/money/2006/jul/11sld2.htm
There's life after Infosys
http://www.business-standard.com/article/technology/there-s-life-after-infosys-109070600021_1.html

A Journey That Was Infosys
http://www.businessworld.in/news/opinion/interviews/a-journey-that-was-infosys/335394/page-1.html
http://solutions.3m.com/wps/portal/3M/en_US/3M-Company/Information/Resources/History/?PC_Z7_RJH9U52300V200IP896S2Q3223000000_assetId=1319210372704
http://ideas.time.com/2012/04/25/why-floundering-is-good/
http://www.universityaffairs.ca/why-students-need-to-fail.aspx
Why Floundering Is Good by Annie Murphy Paul, Times Magazine, April 25, 2012
Why students need to fail: How falling flat on your face may be a terrific way to learn, by Moira MacDonald December 4, 2013
Herring, Hubert. A *History of Latin America From the Beginnings to the Present..* New York: Alfred A. Knopf, 1962
In Head-Hunting, Big Data May Not Be Such a Big Deal, Adam Bryant, New York Times, June 19, 2013

Section VII Managing Failure

http://timesofindia.indiatimes.com/india/India-is-worlds-suicide-capital-with-2-6-lakh-cases/year/articleshow/41737654.cms
ØyvindTønnesson(Ed). *Mahatma Gandhi, the Missing Laureate.* Nobelprize.org Peace Editor, 1998-2000
http://www.nobelprize.org/nobel_prizes/themes/peace/gandhi/
The Risks of RewardsBy Alfie KohnERICDigestDecember 1994
The Peter Principle: Why Things Always Go Wrong. By Laurence J. Peter and Raymond Hull

ACKNOWLEDGEMENTS

As I reflect on the events which made this work possible, I think of the many things which could have gone wrong, but didn't. When I begin to thank people, I find that it is not one individual but a whole community who need to be acknowledged.

I thank Google and its makers and the nameless people who keep the information flowing. Fast.

On a personal front, I remain eternally grateful to my father, Dewan Rajendra Kumar Kochhar, who taught me to think rationally and would have been the happiest person had he lived to see this work.

Failing times are hard times. While winners celebrate, losers look for support within and around themselves. I thank my mother Mohini Kochhar, for always keeping faith in me; Dr. Seema Kochhar and my brother, Dr. Atul Mohan Kochhar, who are pillars of support for the entire family. Without their support and motivation, this work would simply not have been possible.

These people work hard, day in and day out, supporting families, managing relationships and helping communities be better places. They are the linchpins of society, holding up the social machinery. I have much to learn from them.

I thank Aditya and Aryan, who have (sometimes unwittingly), been the source of valuable inputs.

I must express my thanks and gratitude to Chandralekha Maitra, my guide and editor. I thank her for her professionalism in giving shape to this book. And more importantly, for believing in me.

27909176R00117

Made in the USA
Columbia, SC
01 October 2018